Storms
— AND —
Wild Water

Storms
— AND —
Wild Water

Dag Pike

ADLARD COLES NAUTICAL
LONDON

Acknowledgements

Many people have helped with the experiences and photos that have gone into this book. In particular I would like to thank those who have provided their personal reminiscences and also those who have enabled me to get so much practical experience of storms at sea. It has been hard-won experience and sometimes the margins between success and failure have been small but it is something that I would not have missed.

Taking photos of storm seas is never easy and again I am so grateful to those who have taken the photos that appear in this book – they help to bring to life to the reader just what it can be like in storm conditions at sea.

Published by Adlard Coles Nautical
an imprint of
A & C Black Publishers Ltd
36 Soho Square
London W1D 3QY

www.adlardcoles.com

Copyright © Dag Pike 2009

First edition published 2009

ISBN 978-1-4081-1231-1

A CIP catalogue record for this book is available from the British Library.

This book is produced using paper that is made from wood grown in managed, sustainable forests. It is natural, renewable and recyclable. The logging and manufacturing processes conform to the environmental regulations of the country of origin.

Design and typesetting by www.benstudios.co.uk

Typeset in Helvetica Neue 10/14pt

Printed and bound in Singapore by Star Standard Industries Pte Ltd

Note: while all reasonable care has been taken in the publication of this book, the publisher takes no responsibility for the use of the methods or products described in the book.

Contents

The Eye of the Storm

The sea was an oily calm, nearly black in colour where it reflected the distant clouds. There was a feeling of menace in the air, a sense of impending doom. All that day the swell had been building, starting as a low undulation of the sea surface but rapidly growing in size until the serried ranks of the waves marched across the surface of the sea, causing the ship to roll uncomfortably. Then the wind started, disturbing the calm and accentuating the swell, while the clouds grew darker and lower with a strong violet tint. The storm was coming. It was heralded by the waves and the steadily increasing wind, but nothing in the prelude can prepare you for the sheer intensity that follows.

Within hours the mix of rain, spray and wind made the air almost liquid. If you dared to turn your face into the wind, it was difficult to breathe. When you turned your face away it felt like drowning. There was no division between water and air, no division between sea and sky, and the horizon had disappeared in visibility that was now measured in yards. The noise was incredible: the screaming of the wind joining with the crashing of the waves to drown out all other sounds and, seemingly, life itself. It was just as well that we couldn't hear the groans and strains of the hull of the ship as it tried to cope with the ever-changing angle of the waves, because they sound like a death rattle no seaman wants to hear. Everything was basic and elemental, such a mix of noise, movement and emotion that could have heralded the end of the world. It was fearsome and awe-inspiring at the same time, but for the men on board this was just another storm at sea, something to endure for hours or days until peace returned and routine took over again.

This is the working environment of the serious seaman, his 'office desk' where he lives, eats and sleeps in between coping with the extremes of life at sea. In the past a seaman would have been cut off from the rest of the world for weeks

< **The storms clouds gather.**

v **The eye of the storm – a satellite view of a hurricane approaching the Caribbean.**

A stormy sea can be an awe-inspiring sight but danger lurks in every wave.

on end with little or no knowledge of what might happen tomorrow let alone in a week or two. Without any means of communication the sailors had no idea of what might be in store just hours ahead, and the changing weather patterns would be a constant source of worry, probably as much as the fragile state of the ship after months without repair or refit.

To understand and forecast the weather the captain would rely on his experience and what he could see around him. The calm before a storm is a well-recognized phenomenon and even back in the Seventeenth Century the poet John Dryden was writing:

> A horrid stillness first invades the ear,
> And in that silence we the tempest fear

Seamen still talk about storms they have experienced in hushed and reverential terms, affording respect and awe for a situation where the forces of nature can combine to make life on board extremely challenging, and even threaten life itself. In a world that has tamed and controlled so much of nature, a storm at sea still represents nature in the raw, a dramatic demonstration of the uncontrollable power that it can unleash. On land a storm will manifest itself through the effects of the invisible wind tearing at trees and buildings and scooping up anything unsecured. At sea the battleground changes and while the wind can tear at the masts, sails and rigging it is the waves that it generates and the huge amount of energy that they contain that represents the main threat to ships caught out in a storm.

This meeting point of air and sea is one of the most wild and unpredictable arenas in the natural world and this is where the seaman has to pursue his trade, nurse his vessel, negotiate with the wind and the waves and try to find a safe path to salvation at the end of the storm. The wind, in moderate doses, provides the vital means of propulsion for ships and boats. As it rises in strength propulsion comes second and survival takes over.

> **This meeting point of air and sea is one of the most wild and unpredictable arenas in the natural world.**

Storms can cause considerable damage on land but here it is just the strength of the wind that has to be contended with. Out at sea the storm force winds transfer their considerable energy into generating waves and in violent storm winds it is the latent energy in these waves that poses the real threat. In moderate sea conditions this energy remains largely locked in the wave and the particles of water simply go up and down to form the ever-changing shape of the wave. In storms these waves can become unstable. When the wave gradient exceeds an angle of 18°, some or all of the energy contained in the wave is released and the water starts to move forward in a breaking crest, taking tons of water with it. It is this moving water and its huge energy content that threatens the very existence of ships and boats. You only have to look at the huge energy released when a wave breaks on shore to realize what vessels at sea might have to cope with. Seamen talk in awe of fearing for their lives as huge breaking crests bear down on them and, for many, this can be the point of no return, when the ship and its sailors are simply extinguished. Breaking waves can pose a major threat, even with the sophistication of modern ships and boats.

There is no regular pattern to storm waves, and it is these breaking crests that spell danger.

If the waves and the breaking crests followed a regular pattern it might be relatively straightforward to anticipate and cope with them but so much of what transpires in a wild storm is unpredictable. There is nothing here that seems to conform with any recognized law except the applicable laws which say that nothing will be regular and nothing will follow a set pattern. In fact, the only law that seems to apply in these wild waters is Chaos Theory, which suggests that small changes in initial conditions can effect each other exponentially, giving a seemingly random and chaotic outcome.

Waves vary in height and depth, different wave trains interact to create higher waves, the wind can come down on a ship in fierce gusts that are double the strength of the prevailing wind and the visibility can degenerate to the point where it's hard to see and anticipate the next wave. These conditions are just the result of the interaction of the wind and the sea but there is a third dimension that has to be added into the equation – and this is the one that seamen fear the most. The flow of the current or tide, a seemingly harmless low speed flow of water in moderate conditions, can change the whole face of the sea and lead ships and boats to disaster when combined with storm-force winds.

When the wind blows against the tide or the current the waves take on a new dimension, becoming steeper and more aggressive. As the wavelength shortens, the gradient steepens and the wave is much more likely to break, with the crest rolling over and powering down the leeward face of the wave. A ship or boat will find it much harder to fit in between these steeper and higher waves, and the moving water in the breaking crests has the power to do considerable damage and even overwhelm small craft. This is the sailor's nightmare, and the wild breaking seas generated when the wind is against the current have spelt doom to many ships and boats over the centuries man has roamed the world's oceans.

Then there are the 'holes'. These are the deep troughs that lie hidden on the windward side of a wave, only discovered when the vessel comes over the crest to peer into the abyss below. A vessel can literally drop into these holes and there is little time for recovery before the next wave towers above. These potholes of the sea (on a grand scale) are likely to be found more frequently when the wind is blowing against the tide or current in storm conditions, and can overwhelm even large ships. As the powerful Agulhas Current that sweeps around the bottom of South Africa meets the violent westerly winds that cross the Southern Ocean, it creates a notorious breeding ground for holes.

The liner *Edinburgh Castle* reported just such a 'hole' in 1964. In Commodore W S Byles' report he comments: 'And then it happened. Suddenly, having scended as normal, the wave length appeared to be double the normal, about 300ft, so that when the ship pitched she charged, as it were, into a hole in the ocean at an angle of 30° or more, shovelling the next wave on board at a height of 15 to 20ft before she could recover'.

The statistics from the Institute of Oceanography give some indication of the unpredictability of waves at sea. Can you imagine what it is like to be out in a storm where the waves in a rough sea are on average 4 to 5m high? Then along comes a monster wave that is four times this height at close to 20m – over 60ft. Not only is the height of the wave terrifying but its crest will almost certainly break and if that huge wall of water falls down on you, you are in deep trouble. In 60 years at sea I have only encountered three of these monster waves but that was still three too many and they are the most frightening experience you can have on the water. Fortunately, these rogue waves are transient. You may even see them in the distance but they can disappear before they get to you. Equally, they can rear up alongside you without notice and then you're in serious trouble.

> # Then along comes a monster wave that is four times this height at close to 20m – over 60ft.

Many have lost the battle with wild seas. *Virgin Atlantic Challenger* **sinking just south of Ireland, after battling across the Atlantic to try to beat the West/East speed record.**

What is it that has persuaded man to build ships and boats to operate in this hostile environment? What persuades seamen to take on the challenge of storms, when the odds are stacked against them from the start? Initially it was the prospect of finding new lands and riches that motivated the explorers. Then it became the continuing trade with these countries – the prospect of making money is a powerful motivation. The risks were balanced against the rewards that a successful voyage could bring, but even up to the Nineteenth Century the attrition rate was very high.

A storm can be a long and demanding fight for life.

There is also the emotion of a storm, which can become all consuming. A storm can be a long and demanding fight for life. A sailor needs every ounce of skill and stamina to cope with its challenges, he needs a sound ship underneath him and he needs endurance way beyond any demanded on shore. A sailor will run through the whole gamut of emotions before, during and after a storm and these emotions can be just as strong whether you are in a ship or a boat. The storm experience can be particularly intense if you are sailing single-handed. In this situation you literally sink or swim by your own skills and competence. It isn't difficult to see why solo sailors take on the challenge of storms, because it represents possibly the toughest of human endeavours. You are engaged in a fight for survival like nothing else and this fight doesn't just involve using your skills to nurse the boat through the storm, it means coping with the intense physical and mental stress too. To take on such a challenge you need more than just skill – you need passion and emotion to carry you through. It is all too easy to stop and give in, and you need that extra element to drive forward against the odds.

Sleep can be a fitful experience in a storm. The constant motion of the boat or ship makes it difficult but there's also the mental stress that keeps you awake, listening for signs of distress from the boat, worrying about the extra big waves that may lurk out there, thinking about the vulnerability of the mast, rigging and sails. Eventually you sleep through sheer exhaustion but it will never be the deep relaxing sleep that you need. Combine the physical and mental strain of life in a storm and it is so easy to give up and just let events take their course.

Storms at sea can bring out the best and the worst in people but seamen tend to be a special breed that rises to the occasion and

∧ **Riding out a hurricane in the Gulf of Cortez.**

refuses to be beaten, possibly because they have very few options once the storm has started. It is not really a question of fighting a storm because you know that a storm will always keep going long after you have given in. It is more about negotiating with the storm, trying to find a way out of it, protecting the ship or boat and conserving your strength. I am always amazed at how quickly people adapt to dangerous situations. When you sit ashore contemplating the idea of running a boat through a storm the whole concept is totally alien and scary. But out there, there is no choice. You can't run away but you may be able to mitigate the effects of the wild and stormy environment. There are few choices and you must mentally adapt very quickly. This is your new reality and you need to make the best of it.

This is not just the experience of yachtsmen. I've had just the same feeling on a ship riding out a storm – the margins are getting small and life is hanging in the balance. The sailor needs to be mentally strong to cope because this high stress situation can last for hours or even days. Onshore there are risks and dangers, perhaps a narrow escape when you are driving, but these are relatively short-lived, almost transient

> **I experienced storms and hurricanes and the wildest of seas out in the open ocean but I have been lucky enough to have had a reason for doing so for part of the time.**

dangers, and help is usually never far away. When danger and risk last for days with no help at hand, the mental stress is enormous. However, the extreme conditions at the start of a storm can quickly become the new normality. This is your new storm-rocked place of work and you get on with the job with all the skills and experience that you can muster.

In this new environment there are two things that will stand out. The first is the violent movement of the vessel, and you get this on ships and boats. This violent movement can be extremely tiring and you may need to hold on most of the time. The second is the noise and this can reach fever pitch, with the wind shrieking in the rigging and waves crashing in, on and around the vessel. In extreme winds (such as those of a hurricane) the note can go off the scale and this can bring some relief, but you know that the absence of wind noise means that the wind strength is increasing beyond your ability to hear it and you are moving into even more danger. The environment resembles what you imagine the end of the world might be like but your experience should tell you that storms do not last for ever and there has to come a point when things start to get better.

It is a shame that so few people get the chance to experience a storm at sea and even seamen are encouraged to stay in harbour when the storm rages. It is easy and understandable to take the safe option and not go to sea when there is a storm outside, and this is what all the textbooks tell you to do if you have the choice. But out there in a storm you are riding that narrow knife edge between success and failure, between life and death. This is the ultimate thrill ride and it is your skills and endurance that will decide whether you survive or not – it represents a challenge that very little on Earth can equal.

In my 60 years at sea I have probably been through about 30 severe storms. Not only have I experienced storms and hurricanes and the wildest of seas out in the open ocean but I have been lucky enough to have had a reason for doing so for part of the time. My job was to test new designs of lifeboat, to see how they performed in extreme conditions so the lifeboat crews could have confidence in their craft. For me, storms were work – it was a question of waiting for the storm and then going out to sea. This was the most exciting and demanding job ever and it gave me a valuable insight into boats and their behaviour in storm conditions, and how sailors behave when under storm pressure.

I had the benefit of good weather forecasts, so I knew what I was going into. Forecasting storms has now advanced to the point where, if you have the right communications, there should be adequate warning. This should enable most ships and yachts to avoid them altogether, or at least avoid the worst parts, because some storms are so extensive that there may be little chance of total escape. Slower yachts might have some difficulty in escaping and these are likely to be the same vessels that lack the good communications necessary for adequate warnings. Despite the advances in forecasting, ships and yachts still encounter storms and many do not come out unscathed. Even the biggest modern ships can get into trouble in violent storms so size is no guarantee of survival. Even in the modern world storms still present an untamed source of wild and damaging weather that demonstrates man's inability to control nature.

A passenger ship heads into storm conditions where easing the speed is the only way to achieve a comfortable ride for the people on board.

Forecasting Storms

No navigator would dream of going to sea today without a weather forecast. Indeed, it has now become a legal requirement in many countries to obtain a weather forecast before leaving harbour. It sounds so obvious, logical and seamanlike that I find it surprising that it has to be made mandatory. Yet, 70 years ago you would have struggled to find a forecast to tell you what was going to happen over the next 24 hours and, if you were out at sea, getting a good forecast was next to impossible. Early warning of the approach of a storm is vital to safety and forecasts are now available for several days ahead. Combined with modern weather routeing, it should be possible to avoid storms altogether.

For hundreds of years seamen went to sea without any weather forecasts. They might have delayed departure because the prevailing weather did not look promising or because the winds were foul but, once they were out at sea, they had to take whatever was on offer. Experienced seamen would get to know the signs of an approaching storm and would batten down the hatches and prepare for it. However, knowing where a storm was located and where it was heading would largely be intelligent guesswork. The only forecasting methods that were available to seamen relied on what they could see happening around them: the clouds, the rain, the wind and, best of all, the swell. Experience with these immediate weather signs might herald an approaching storm but by then it would be close and too late to take avoiding action.

The swell on the surface of the sea provided the best indication of an approaching storm, perhaps giving 24 hours' notice of strong winds. Swell is the long, low waves generated by a wind that may be some distance away and the aftermath of wind-generated

> **The explosive force of waves is captured in this photo. A captain needs to nurse his ship through these conditions to reduce the stress on the hull.**

> **If the wind increases much more, this yacht will have to shorten sail.**

waves that remain when the wind is no longer feeding them energy. The swell can travel both in advance of a storm and after it and a low, lazy swell that might disturb the surface could result from a severe storm 1,000 miles away, although it would normally be much closer. The higher the swell the closer the storm so a lively swell a metre or two high could be a good indication that a storm was lurking not far over the horizon. The direction of the swell would also give a rough idea of where the storm was located, as the swell would fan out from the storm centre. A swell coming from directly ahead would mean the ship was heading straight towards a storm.

With experience, swell could give vital early warning although maybe not with enough accuracy to allow the ship to take evasive action. As the storm got closer the cloud formations could also help and there are regular and identifiable progressions of cloud formations that herald the approach of many storms. Tropical storms can often be identified over 100 miles away from the cloud that spins off the top of the storm at very high levels but for storms in temperate latitudes it is the clouds associated with the various frontal systems that give clues about the approaching storm.

Even back in 650 BC the Babylonians were using cloud formations to predict the weather. Astrology was also used, the thinking being that the movements of the stars and planets had some influence on the weather. The Greek philosopher Aristotle wrote his treatise, *Meteorologica*, in the Third Century BC, in which he explained his theories about various weather phenomena, but it was not until the Fifteenth and Sixteenth Centuries that instruments were developed to measure weather phenomena, such as the temperature and barometric pressure.

By the Seventeenth Century the relationship between atmospheric pressure and the wind had been noticed but knowledge of general weather patterns and the highs and lows of the weather was still a long way off. Initially, barometer readings could only be taken on land so there were vast expanses of the world (the oceans) where the weather was still a mystery. It took another century before barometers were developed that could be taken to sea on ships, opening the door to an early warning system for storms. It was not just the actual reading of the barometer that was important but the rise and fall and the speed of movement that were indicative of weather changes. A sharp drop in pressure was a pretty sure indication that a storm was imminent but it did not show where the storm was in relation to the ship. However, taken with the indications from the swell and from clouds, the mariner had a better idea of the situation than before. Admiral Fitzroy's Storm Barometer became a vital piece of equipment on ships and the change of the barometer reading was a standard entry in every logbook.

Storms were such devastating events on land and around the coasts that the focus of weather forecasting was always towards what was happening on land. The importance of forecasting for ships at sea was recognized when Capt (later Admiral) Fitzroy was appointed to head the British Meteorological Office when it was set up in 1854. The storm cone warning systems for shipping and seamen were established along the coasts, mainly at Coastguard stations. A chart covering the years 1873 to 1887 shows a direct correlation between the number of storm warning stations and the value of shipping, losses around the British coasts, demonstrating the benefits of this system.

The Met Office set up the first storm warning service in 1861 but it was mainly of benefit to mariners in inshore waters. It was made possible by the development of the electric telegraph, which could bring weather information in to a central point where it could be processed and sent out again in the form of warnings. This was one of the early benefits of electronic communications but it relied on visual signs to communicate the warnings to shipping, so it was only of value near the coasts. It was not until 1911 that a storm warning system was established to cover the north Atlantic. The Cunard Line ships were receiving daily weather reports by radio before this and 1905 saw the first weather reports coming in from ships so that the forecaster had a better idea of what was happening over the oceans.

One of the primary reasons for the establishment in the US of the National Weather Service in 1870 was the heavy shipping losses on the

V Even with today's technology, it is impossible to forecast waves like this.

stormy Great Lakes. A study for 1868 claimed that there were 1,914 vessel casualties (resulting in the loss of 321 lives and 105 ships) from storms on the lakes that were right in the path of many of the severe storms sweeping across the American continent. Because it was possible to get weather observations from land stations around the lakes, a reliable warning system could be developed.

There is no point having a storm warning system unless the warnings can be passed to users, and for ships this came about with the development of radio communication. All weather forecasting depends on getting readings of the prevailing weather from observation stations and putting these together in the form of a synoptic chart that gives a picture of the isobars and other weather information in the familiar weather chart. One of the problems with European weather is that forecasting it accurately depends on knowing what is going on across the wide open Atlantic Ocean because most of the weather comes from that direction. This meant relying on weather information sent in from observing ships and, as radio communications improved, the value of these ship readings increased. The First World War put many of these on hold but after the war the Bergen School of Meteorology

V Although satellites can't look into the future, satellite technology has helped forecasters to predict storms.

developed a new storm analysis technique. It incorporated the movements of frontal systems (that would herald wind direction and strength changes) as well as tracking the main low-pressure areas, and this greatly helped in forecasting storms.

The increase in air travel across the oceans gave ocean weather forecasting a strong impetus and the Second World War also helped to focus on the value of good forecasting for shipping. However, forecasting still relied heavily on the skills and experience of individual forecasters. It was these forecasters who drew up the synoptic charts and the weather forecast was based largely on their interpretation of these charts. Two developments then took place that were to change the whole approach to storm forecasting and greatly improve the accuracy of the forecast.

In 1961 the weather satellite *Tiros 1* was launched, the first of many dedicated to monitoring the changing weather patterns around the globe giving the forecasters a bird's eye view of them. Nothing could escape these satellites and they gave a global picture of the changing atmospheric conditions, almost in real time – a significant improvement from just relying on the information from ship reports. These reports are still required to verify the satellite information and, of course, the satellites cannot measure the atmospheric pressure, probably the most vital single piece of weather information. What the satellites do best is covering areas of ocean where ships are sparse and they can detect and monitor embryo tropical storms before ship reports find them. The satellite information is a vital tool for the forecaster but, of course, it only shows what has happened or what is happening and it cannot look into the future.

> *Satellite information is a vital tool for the forecaster but, of course, it only shows what has happened or what is happening and it cannot look into the future.*

The other significant development was that of the computer. Today, weather forecasters use some of the most powerful computers in the world to develop their predictions. These computers hold all the recorded historical weather patterns, their changes and developments and these show how the weather has developed in a particular set of circumstances. When a new set of weather information is put into the computer it searches for matching patterns from the past and uses these to show what might be expected to happen in the future. This is what a human forecaster would have tried to do, but without the huge mass of historical data to help him.

The computer gets it right most of the time and from this we get fairly reliable forecasts of storms, so we can be prepared and possibly take avoiding action. However, the computer can fall down when extremes of weather take place. Such extremes are rare, so the historical records do not always have enough data to forecast them. A forecaster might be wary if the computer shows up the possibility of an extreme type of storm and he might discount it, as forecaster Michael Fish did when violent storms were actually taking place in the English Channel in 1987. Equally, the computer might not show up the extremes and so the mariner does not get a warning about what might be severe conditions. The computer only runs a new forecast every 12 hours in most cases and then it takes perhaps 6 hours to assess, forecast and disseminate the weather, so short-term violent changes could be missed within that time. We are still a long way from knowing exactly what the weather will do and there will always be changes that will catch out the mariner. While forecasts now stretch five or more days ahead there are no guarantees that what is forecast will actually happen and it is when the weather becomes extreme that forecasting can become more difficult and unreliable.

We have no means of controlling and managing the extremes of weather in the modern world so the best we can hope for is to try to forecast what the weather will do so that ships and yachts can escape the worst of the extremes. Weather routeing is now used by many ships to find the optimum route through the changing weather patterns. The routeing is done partly by computer and partly by the human forecaster, with the aim of finding the best course with the least disruption in terms of loss of speed, burning the minimum of fuel or, where sensitive cargoes are being carried, finding the most comfortable route. In this way ships are often able to avoid storms, although when a storm is extensive it is unlikely that it can be avoided altogether.

Weather routeing can be more sophisticated for yachts, and for yachts participating in long-distance ocean races, it is a vital part of the challenge. Here, the requirement is to find the best route to optimize the speed towards the destination, balancing this against the deteriorating sea conditions as winds increase, which could slow down or damage a yacht. Once again, the computer can get it right most of the time but the man at the helm is still the one making the final decision.

We now have very sophisticated weather information and forecasting, and this should reduce the chance of getting into a severe storm. However, good weather information demands good communications

and that is not always possible within the confines of a small craft. Any seaman has to remember that these are only forecasts and there is no certainty that a forecast is going to be right. In many cases there can be a vagueness in the forecast with the predicted wind strength covering a range of speeds, suggesting that the forecaster is not entirely sure of what will happen. It only takes quite minor changes in the weather patterns to cause significant changes in the wind strength so the forecaster has to hedge his bets. The man on the spot still has a role to play and, while he may get plenty of advice, he is the only one who can see and feel the vessel and the prevailing conditions. Storms can have a nasty habit of changing in the short term in a way that cannot be forecast so when trying to anticipate the weather there is no room for complacency.

Clouds can provide the navigator with a short-term view of the future.

Ships in
Storms

Even in Biblical times ships were being buffeted by storms. *The Acts of the Apostles* contains a description of St Paul as a prisoner on a ship sailing to Italy from Israel, beset by a storm for 14 days and only surviving through the power of prayer. Back in those days and for centuries afterwards storms were looked on as God's retribution for misdeeds. Many large naval ships carried clerics to help ward off impending storms and seamen would pray for wind so they could make progress but also when there was too much wind. It was a vital element of navigation and the *Book of Common Prayer* of 1692 has two prayers for use in storms at sea.

Early ships could only make progress when the wind was more or less abaft the beam so adverse winds were a real problem. It is not difficult to see why the sailors soon learnt where the general wind patterns would be favourable when sailing across the open oceans. The pattern of trade winds that can be found over the major oceans provided the sort of steady sailing winds that allowed the ships to make good progress towards their destinations. Even as early as the Columbus voyages of discovery they knew that there was a general westwards wind flow across the lower part of the north Atlantic, what we now call the trade winds. For the journey home the ships would head back further north where there was a reciprocal wind flowing generally from west to east but on this more northerly route there was a much higher risk of storms.

The main risk to these sailing ships was storms. We tend to think of these as being predictable inconveniences but to those early sailors they were life or death events and they could come with very little warning. By the time the captain became aware of an impending storm there would be little chance of avoiding it. He could only hope for enough warning to get the ship battened down and the sails furled to weather the storm.

Storm conditions can put a heavy stress on ships and their crews.

A Spanish galleon blown ashore in a hurricane off the Florida coast.

> *The older sailing ships would not sail very close to the wind, perhaps no more than 70° either side of the direction from which the wind was blowing.*

I cannot begin to imagine what it must have been like to have no warning of an approaching storm and no measure of what its intensity might be. If things went wrong and the ship was damaged, perhaps losing its masts or its steering, there was no one out there to help, no lifeboat to come to the rescue, no way of calling for assistance. You had to fight your own battles and if the ship foundered there would be no one to record the event. The chances of getting away from a wreck in the ship's boat were small because it was likely to be the first thing to get smashed by waves coming on deck. Living or dying was entirely a matter of seamanship skills, nursing the ship through the storm and, hopefully, coming out the other side. It is not difficult to see why prayer was considered a vital ally in this situation.

The pictures of those early sailing ships give little indication of their size but, by modern standards, they were very tiny for ocean voyages. Each of the ships in Columbus's fleet was less than 100ft (30m) in length, minute for an ocean voyage and crowded with crew and possibly passengers. If the captain was lucky he would have a soundly-constructed ship with less chance of failure of the hull and rigging. Breakage of any part of a ship, perhaps a vital piece of rigging failing under the stress of storm winds, could lead it down the path of escalating disaster and eventual foundering. As trade developed, many unsuitable ships were pressed into service. These ships may have been built soundly at the beginnings of their lives but time could take its toll on the structure, and rotten planking or framing could provide the sort of weakness that storm-force winds could so easily exploit. Such high-risk voyages were unlikely to attract the best quality crews, and if ever a high level of seamanship skills was required it would be in handling a sailing ship in a storm.

It is difficult to comprehend how trade developed to the extent it did but the rewards of a successful voyage were high enough to make the risks acceptable. These risks lay mainly in the chances of encountering a storm and, if we take the Atlantic as an example, there was the risk of encountering a hurricane on the outward voyage when ships were following the trade wind route across the Atlantic from east to west. For six months of the year hurricanes can form over the eastern side of the Atlantic and travel west towards the Americas. By the time a ship discovered that it was in a hurricane there was no way out and it had to

A watery view through the bridge windows of this ship pitching in a storm.

try to weather it. Those that succumbed to the storm would leave no trace. Those that survived were unlikely to come through the storm unscathed but, by living to tell their tale, the knowledge and experience would be developed slowly so that mariners would eventually have better information with which to plan future action when they encountered one. It was painfully-won experience but it would be centuries before warning systems would become available to enable ships to take avoiding action.

It is hard to understand how the crews of the ships on these early voyages could set out with such a small degree of certainty that they would ever return. Whilst they might have been persuaded that the captain knew where he was going and the level of risk involved, the captain and his officers must have known from experience that the risks were high. One can only assume that the rewards were greater than the perceived dangers and these would justify undertaking such high risk voyages. As trade developed and navigation skills improved, some of the problems were removed but there was still the possibility of storms as the great unknown in any ocean voyage right up to the Twentieth Century. The statistics do not make good reading. In just one decade in the 1860s 2,500 ships in the British fleet sank in deep water and we must assume that many of these were lost in storms. Looking at it another way, more than half of all the sailing ships operating in British waters were lost at sea during the Eighteenth and Nineteenth Centuries.

The main priority for any sailing ship captain preparing to meet a storm will be to try to gain as much sea room as possible. This is not a problem on the open sea, where there are miles of open space, but, when sailing close to land, sea room can be a vital commodity. The older sailing ships would not sail very close to the wind, perhaps no more than 70° either side of the direction from which the wind was blowing. Under storm conditions this might be reduced to 90° either side of the wind because of the leeway, which would severely restrict the ship's ability to manoeuvre away from the land. If the wind was blowing towards the shore there would be a serious risk of the ship being blown ashore too. The situation could be even more serious if the ship was in a bay with the wind blowing onshore because it would lack the ability to sail clear of the adjoining headlands. The Bay of Biscay got its evil reputation for this reason, with ships trapped in the bay by a series of westerly gales and lacking the ability to sail out.

Equally serious was the ability of a ship to survive a storm without any failures. Even those ships that were very strongly built would start to 'work' in a seaway. A wooden hull structure is not rigid and the very slight movement between the timbers could open up leaks when the ship was under stress. The hull was rarely fully watertight and in a storm the pumps would have to be manned frequently to keep the water levels inside the hull under control. Older ships could flex even more and if they had not been well maintained there was always the risk of the caulking between the planks failing or, worse still, the hull fastenings pulling out. An Italian commentator, talking about the storms that ships endured, said: 'Survivors would tell how strong wooden hulls were split open by the waves, of how towering masts had blown away like straws while the air and water merged together under the storm.'

A storm tends to find the weak points of a ship and starts it on a downhill slope towards disaster. If the leaking of the hull gets worse the crew have to focus on that and perhaps not give other aspects of the ship the attention required. It is the mast and rigging of a sailing ship that are perhaps most vulnerable in a storm and on old ships this was all rope and wood, materials that could deteriorate with age.

Ship owners would also put pressure on captains to overload their ships, to carry as much cargo as possible in order to maximize the profit. A deeply laden ship is more at risk of foundering in a storm but it was not until the late 1800s that the Plimsoll Line was made law by Parliament in Britain, dictating the depth to which a ship could be loaded. It was a step forward but not the full solution.

This small naval ship is battling its way through a storm in the Bering Sea, where the margin between success and failure can be terrifyingly small.

If these sailing ships did sink there would be little chance of survival. Virtually nothing in the way of safety and survival equipment was carried: no lifejackets, no liferafts, no lifeboats, the only hope of survival resting on the ship's boats or clinging to floating debris. The boats were basically open rowing boats and even if they could be launched in a storm when a ship was sinking they did not offer much more hope of survival than the ship itself. It was not just the crews that were at risk in storms. Passenger travel by sailing ship was well established even back in the Sixteenth Century. Over 600 passengers were lost on a Spanish galleon sailing back from Cuba and 2,000 were lost when a fleet of troop ships foundered off Canada.

Storms at sea have shaped history – it was not just the British fleet under Sir Francis Drake that destroyed the Spanish Armada. After Drake had attacked the Spanish, bad weather in the English Channel forced them up channel and then they continued around the north of Scotland to find their long way home. Only a few made it, with many being wrecked in storms off the Scottish and Irish coasts.

The great storm of 1703 that hit the English Channel showed just how vulnerable shipping was. The storm lasted for eight days and during that time the Royal Navy lost 13 ships and it is reckoned that over 1,500 seaman drowned. This was the same storm that destroyed the first Eddystone Lighthouse, taking with it its builder, Henry Winstanley, and five others. Shoals and land added to the risks and dangers.

Compared with the perceived security of the modern world, life on those early sailing ships was a pretty basic existence. The crews could set out on a voyage with only a 50 per cent chance of returning. As the design of sailing ships improved and concepts like the speedy clipper ships were developed, the risks from storms changed. As the quality and the sailing abilities of the ships increased the risk of failure reduced, but speed and schedules then came into the reckoning. In their rush to get their precious cargoes home the pressure was on to keep going in storm conditions, to maintain speed at all costs so, in many ways, the stresses on the ships and gear were just as high and the danger increased. Now the captains had to tread that narrow line between success and failure and in most cases you don't know where the line is until you cross it. There are so many unknowns in storm conditions that the captain's judgement is a critical aspect of survival.

Sail gave way to steam, and ships then had the ability to make good progress to windward. This gave a lot more safety in storm conditions and there was no longer quite the same dread of a lee shore. However, weather forecasting was still in its infancy and shipping still got little or no warning of a storm ahead. The introduction of steam also meant that ships could take direct routes to their destinations so there was even less excuse for delay. Now ships were expected to keep to schedules and, once again, ships' captains were forced to choose between making the best progress to the destination and easing the ship through a storm. Passenger ships were particularly vulnerable in this respect, partly because the speeds were higher and partly because the schedules were tighter. Slowing down was an option taken reluctantly, and there are many tales of ships being damaged as they forced their ways through stormy seas. With their fine bows, designed to cleave the waves at speed, there was less buoyancy to rise to a wave and it was often the bridge front that took the full brunt of a wave impact. The *Lusitania* was a liner that had its bridge wrecked, even though it was located 80ft (24m) above the sea, when it was struck by a big wave on the Atlantic run.

As weather forecasting improved and radio communications allowed warnings to be passed to shipping, the ships' captains were better prepared to cope with severe weather but they were still challenged by the need to keep to time. While busy routes such as the north Atlantic were well-provided with weather forecasts, in the more remote oceans ships still had to rely on their own resources to forecast the advent of storms. Even in the 1950s in the Pacific we encountered a hurricane that was only forecast after we were in the storm. Ship designers also have to strike a balance between making a ship as efficient as possible so that it can earn money and making it strong enough to cope with violent storms. As recently as the 1950s a ship would rarely come through a violent storm unscathed and, whilst the damage might not

have been life-threatening, it served as a constant reminder of the power contained in storm waves.

To see portholes smashed by wave impact, a metal guard over the gear wheels of the anchor capstan bent in and out of the teeth of the gear, a metal lifeboat squashed flat and the cargo derricks bent when the lashings of a deck cargo gave way were all reminders of the sheer power of storm waves.

The sheer power of storm seas can make ships vulnerable.

Storm damage is a frequent occurrence, particularly to container ships where the cargo is piled high on deck.

On modern ships you would think that this problem had been solved. Tank testing of ship models, computer design and long experience of what works and what doesn't in storm conditions should have given ship designers the knowledge to design and build ships that can cope with anything the sea might throw at them. That would be possible if the captain of the ship could dictate the speed and course best suited to the conditions and if the designer was free to dictate the shape and style of the ship. However, both designer and captain are required to perform, the designer to make the ship as efficient as possible and the captain to maintain schedules irrespective of the sea conditions, and under these pressures storms continue to pose a threat to shipping.

Storm damage is a frequent occurrence, particularly to container ships where the cargo is piled high on deck and the ship is expected to maintain a schedule to within the hour so that it can guarantee its berth at the destination port. The captain has to perform and most of the time it works. Weather routeing for the ship is expected to take it clear of storms and allow it to maintain its speed but the container ship *Napoli* was an example of a ship being driven into a storm and the stress on the hull going beyond the design limits.

Any ship can only take so much in storm conditions before something breaks. The designer probably has some idea where the limits are but nearly every ship goes to sea largely untested. There is no attempt to take a new ship out in severe conditions to see if it meets its design criteria. It is left to the captain to work things out for himself, to get a feel for how the ship is performing in adverse conditions and to make a judgement about what is the best solution. You won't find books written about this subject and a captain is given little or no information about how his ship will cope with storms.

The vast majority of ships that sail the world's oceans today are powered by single engines and have single steering systems. A failure of one of these components renders a ship uncontrollable so it ends up drifting, the captain can no longer guide his vessel through the storm and trying to effect repairs can be a nightmare on a rolling ship. It is hard to understand why the legislating authorities do not insist on two engines and alternative steering systems or, if they won't, you might think that the insurance companies would. After all, the lesson has been learned on small craft where twin engines are now the norm. Insurance companies seem to accept the storm risk to shipping and manage it by setting their premiums accordingly. The authorities are starting to sit up and take notice but only because of the risk of extensive pollution from a casualty, not from the risk to the lives of the crews on board.

Passenger ships are not immune to storms and the list of storm disasters involving these ships is frightening. The *Princess of the Stars* put to sea in a typhoon in the Philippines, lost engine power, drifted helplessly ashore and capsized with the loss of over 800 people in 2008. Was this 24,000-ton ship forced to sail into the typhoon in order to maintain a schedule? Just 38 people survived this disaster. Over 1,000 people were reported to have drowned when a ferry capsized in a storm off the Gambia in west Africa in 2002. The ferry *Estonia* was one of the worst passenger ship disasters in the Western world when she capsized and sank in a storm in the Baltic in 1994 with the loss of 852 lives. The bow doors were the initial failure that led to disaster and you have to wonder about the design criteria that allows bow doors to be fitted to a ship that was to operate in stormy seas. The bow of a ship is the part that takes the maximum stress in a storm and this is not the place to cut holes in the structure.

As passenger ships get bigger and bigger, some carrying over 5,000 people, the risk of a major storm disaster increases. These ships operate in hurricane-prone waters in the Caribbean and whilst, in theory, a ship would have adequate warning of storms and be able to take avoiding action, history shows that there will always be the risk of taking chances with the weather to maintain schedules. These are the curse of modern shipping and they can force captains into making decisions that go against the principles of sound seamanship. Then again, storms can be worse than forecast and there are extreme waves lurking out there. A captain may find a speed for his ship that works well with most waves but it only takes one extreme wave to cause severe damage.

The design of ships is also bucking the trend of sound, seamanlike designs. Modern passenger ships take the superstructure right forward so that the bridge is right in the bow. This is not the best situation if the ship is caught out in a storm. The cruise ship *Pacific Star* suffered considerable damage to her bridge when she encountered a storm in the Pacific that was apparently much more severe than forecast. The *Pacific Sun* was damaged and passengers injured in a storm in the same area north of New Zealand. Perhaps it is time to return to more

It only takes a failure of one component on a ship to make it vulnerable in storm seas.

sensible ship designs where there is less emphasis on profits and more on seaworthiness but, because this will only follow legislation these days, how do you legislate for such a change?

It seems that the designers of modern ships are taking chances in order to maximize their viability. They are not designed to cope with the worst that the sea can throw at them any longer and they are instead expected to be able to take avoiding action to escape the worst of storms. Ship handling in open seas is given very little coverage in literature and, as ships grow in size, the crews are more distanced from outside conditions. One captain I know on a very large container ship walked to the bow twice a day so that he could get a better feel for how the ship was relating to the prevailing seas, something he could not do from his enclosed bridge high above the waves.

> *It seems that the designers of modern ships are taking chances in order to maximize their viability.*

The logical way to deal with storm conditions is to slow down and to find a course and speed where the ship can cope with the conditions without too much stress on the hull and components. A good captain will know the best tactics to reduce the strain on the ship and its cargoes or passengers and these will vary from ship to ship. Dodging into the head sea or better still heading a little off the direct direction of the waves can often be the best course, but each ship will have a different best heading and this can vary with the loading of the ship and whether it has sensitive cargo on board. When I was at sea many years ago we had the luxury of time to find a suitable heading and speed to nurse the ship through a storm but that does not happen these days and ships, particularly container ships, can be very sensitive to storm damage because of the huge amounts of cargo on deck. These container cargoes are often stacked like a pack of cards – take away just one container and the whole lot can collapse and fall overboard.

Many ships these days use ship routeing to avoid storms and thus the need to slow down. Ship routeing can be done on board provided that suitable weather forecasts are available for a few days ahead. Specialist companies also provide ship routeing services, where the characteristics of the ship and the anticipated weather conditions are fed into a computer, which then comes up with the best possible course. Most of the time they get it right but when you come up against a situation where a major storm is approaching a key location such as the entrance to the English Channel, the options for routeing can disappear and the ship has to cope with the prevailing conditions because there is no alternative.

Ships have always had to negotiate with storm conditions, avoiding them if possible or edging their way through. But the time pressures on modern shipping do not always allow for negotiation and yet the ships are not necessarily designed to cope with storms. Add to this the fact that ships go to sea without any serious testing of their seaworthiness and you have a recipe for continuing storm disasters at sea. It may only take one bigger than normal wave to cause the damage that can then lead to an escalating disaster situation, and as we will see in the chapter on Extreme Waves, those bigger than normal waves are out there.

Superyachts may appear to be all glamour and style, but many are designed to cope with rough seas.

MOONEN YACHTS

Small Craft in Storms

It was **Joshua Slocum** who began it all by sailing round the world in his yacht, *Spray*, starting in 1895. As far as is known this was the first time that a yacht had set off on a world cruise single-handed under sail, and the story still whets the appetite of armchair sailors. In his book of the voyage Slocum shrugs off storms and talks about brewing coffee and an Irish stew over a wood fire at the height of a storm after he had first entered the Pacific through the Strait of Magellan. *Spray* was blown back towards the dangerous rocks and channels towards Cape Horn in a storm; as Slocum put it, 'This was the greatest adventure of my life.'

Despite all his skills and seamanship Slocum eventually disappeared on a voyage from the US down to South America in 1909 when he was 65. Many would argue that this would have been the way he would have wanted to go but his memory as one of the greatest of the single-handers lives on. Many have followed in his footsteps and sailing on long adventurous voyages in yachts has now become such a regular occurrence that it no longer hits the headlines. Such sailing used to put yachts out of reach of weather forecasts and the skipper of the yacht back in the same position as the old sailing ships, relying entirely on his or her own resources to cope with whatever the weather brought in the way of storms. This was the challenge of these open ocean voyages; you were out there on your own, far from help and assistance and you had to find a solution to every problem and challenge or die in the attempt.

It requires a special sort of person to take on this challenge and much of the inspiration comes from Slocum, who showed just how self-reliant you can be. I have done several crossings in small craft and I know just how lonely it can be in the vastness of the ocean. You are humbled by the sheer scale of it and your craft is tiny, especially when amongst the big storm waves. This feeling must be even stronger when you are out there single-handed with no one to help solve problems. Some would argue that it is better to be on your own so you have no one to argue with, but in storm conditions fatigue is an ever-present problem for the single-hander.

In the open ocean there is probably not quite the same need to keep a lookout as there is in the crowded waters near shore but collision is

Testing conditions for the Cork Pilot Boat in the entrance to Cork Harbour.

an ever-present risk. Those who participate in the Single-Handed Trans-Atlantic Race are at high risk from collision because you just cannot be on deck for days on end and the Atlantic is a busy place. The risk of collision is much higher under storm conditions when the visibility can deteriorate considerably and your focus is on surviving the storm. A storm can present a major challenge for a single-hander with the possibility of lasting for days at a time. It is when you combine the extreme fatigue generated by a storm with the mental stress of knowing that any moment might be your last if an extreme wave comes along that worrying about other shipping takes a back seat. In storm conditions it can take a supreme effort just to do the simplest task and the temptation to batten down and let events take their course can be very strong.

For the adventurous cruising yachtsman, storms have been an ever-present danger that can heighten the experience

There are classic books written about how to cope with storms at sea, and *Heavy Weather Sailing* leads the list. These books give personal experiences of those caught out in storms at sea and lots of advice about the different courses of action to take in different conditions. *Heavy Weather Sailing* is a book for the armchair sailor to gain a vicarious experience of storms at sea but it also serves as the Bible for those who are actually going ocean voyaging. You can read about the options and the tactics others have adopted. When you get caught out in a storm they can give a clue but in the end you have to find your own solutions.

For the adventurous cruising yachtsman, storms have been an ever-present danger that can heighten the experience but at the same time present a considerable risk. Cruising into some of the more remote parts of the ocean can mean that there is a reduced chance of rescue if things do go wrong and the forecasting of storms may not be as reliable as in those parts of the ocean where traffic is dense. In many ways these lonely yacht voyages are like turning back the clock to the days of the early sailing ships and there is actually not a lot of difference in the sizes of the vessels. It is interesting to note that most of the stories about survival from extreme storms have occurred in times when the weather forecasting was less precise and when communications onboard small craft were less reliable. Today the storm experience appears to be reduced as good forecasting and reliable communications mean that a yacht should have ample warning of an approaching storm and should thus have time to take avoiding action or at least prepare the yacht.

In storms even the simplest tasks are a challenge. Francis Chichester noted: 'It took me an hour to dress, make tea, collect my tools and make a start. The rolling was frightful and I felt as feeble as a half-dead mouse.' Alec Rose felt much the same, saying: 'Even the smallest job has to be a thought-out plan of action, taking four times as long as usual.' Most single-handers report on the extreme difficulty of using a sextant to fix the position when the boat is rolling. Today, with satellite position fixing, this is no longer a problem, but the extreme movement of small boats remains.

In some ways a yacht is better off than a ship in storm conditions. A yacht is small enough to bob on the surface like a cork. Ships do not have the same resilience and their size can make them span successive waves so the ship can find itself going up when it should be coming down. In stormy seas it is easy to imagine that the best course of action is simply to batten down and let the boat ride the waves but this ignores the fact that some of the waves will be breaking.

In regular waves the water simply goes up and down and the yacht will go up and down with it. Breaking waves are a different matter because, once the crest starts to break because the wave has become unstable, the latent energy in the wave is released and the water rushes forward down the slope with considerable force. In big seas this can engulf a yacht and many are the tales of a yacht being rolled over by breaking waves. This sort of capsize can be devastating, often resulting in the loss of the mast and damage on deck. Water may even enter the hull unless it is very secure and there can be an indescribable mess inside as everything loose gets mixed up. The real risk in this scenario is that the crew will be injured. After a roll of this type recovery can be a slow process. The yacht may be upright again but you are on the downward slope to disaster as you try to recover. It would be rare for just one wave to be breaking and one capsize can often follow another.

This vulnerability to rolling comes when the yacht is lying 'a-hull' and is beam-on to the waves. Even with no sail up a yacht will still make way through the water under bare poles so another option is to run before the seas, sometimes towing warps to slow the progress downwind. There is a risk here

On a sailboat, close-hauled into a strong wind.

of pitch-poling, capsizing stern over bow. This can happen when the bow is buried in the slope of the next wave with a breaking wave coming up behind. This is a frightening situation and I have come close to experiencing this in an 80ft (24m) catamaran in the middle of the Atlantic. We were running under bare poles in 90 knots of wind, still doing 11 knots even with warps out astern. The bow buried and you could feel the boat check its speed. Then the bow kept going down and I was up to my chest in water, standing at the mast. At an angle of about 45° the wave passed under the hull and we came back onto an even keel. It was a close call because if a multihull capsizes or pitch-poles there is no coming back.

Another dimension to the danger to yachts in storms comes when a yacht is close to land. You have a much better chance of surviving the storm if you have all the sea room you need but close to land or shoals your options may be limited. Being caught out in a storm when the wind is blowing towards the land has been the nightmare for sailors since the beginning of time. On a yacht you then have to sail to make progress to windward and all the time the wind is trying to force you towards the shore. It can be a mighty battle and if you are sailing single-handed you are in for a real struggle, fighting with fatigue as well as the storm itself.

Ernest Shackleton experienced this in his heroic voyage in the open ship's boat, *James Caird,* when he undertook an 800 mile voyage in the south Atlantic to bring help to his stranded crew. The worst part of the voyage was making the landfall in South Georgia when a storm was blowing towards the shore. 'Our need for water and rest was well nigh desperate but to have attempted a landing would have been suicidal.' They were on a dead lee shore and had to try to claw their way off whilst, all the time, the boat was filling with water. With the thunder of the breakers in their ears and disaster looming they were saved by a sudden change of wind.

One of the major risks in storm conditions comes if the boat gets damaged. You have enough of a challenge on your hands if the boat is sound and everything is working as it should but damage takes your focus away from coping with the conditions. Most of the tales

> **Safe from the storm? A disabled yacht alongside (and in the lea of) a rescue ship in storm conditions.**

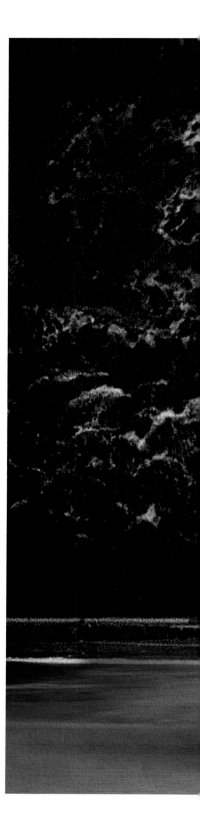

Fishing boats put themselves at considerable risk trying to get in one more haul before the onset of a storm.

about yachtsmen getting into serious trouble in storms stem from some form of boat damage as the start of the descent into deep trouble. The same applies to ships, of course, and any damage tends to limit your course of action. On the same catamaran that nearly pitch-poled we found cracks starting to form around the hull by the cockpits. Instead of continuing with our record-breaking Atlantic crossing attempt, we now had to nurse the boat home. Despite our best efforts, the cracks got worse and when they were halfway round the hull it was time to call for help before the boat broke in two, when we would have been at very serious risk.

Ocean-going yachtsmen should be able to cope with minor damage and have the means on board to sort things out. Even when the damage is more serious, like losing your mast, a jury rig can be fixed with what remains. However, like our hull cracks on that catamaran, there are some things that just cannot be fixed at sea. When Tony Bullimore lost his keel in the Southern Ocean, there was no going back. Multihulls cannot be righted once they have capsized and some of the modern long distance racing yachts with their wide beams are more stable upside down, even with their keels attached, and so will not come back if they capsize. If a yacht is going to go sailing across the oceans it has to be strong and designed to survive to give the crew a chance. The approach to the design of modern racing yachts that sail into the deepest oceans has changed.

Yachts were racing across the oceans as far back as 1866, when the first Atlantic race was held. This was for big yachts, well over 100ft (30m) in length, but it set a pattern that was to lead to a regular Atlantic race starting in 1950 and the single-handed Trans-Atlantic Race in 1960. It was these latter races that took what were virtually standard designs into the hot fire of Atlantic competition. These boats and their crews had tough races and had to weather Atlantic storms, sailing against the prevailing winds, but in the main they made the crossing without high drama.

Compare this with the yachts that race in the many ocean and round the world races that take place today. The standard designs have been replaced by dedicated racing machines – and this is where the trouble starts. For a yacht to have the best high speed performance it needs to be as light at possible and lightweight means paring down the strength to what the designer thinks is the acceptable minimum. The trouble is that yacht design is a complex subject and the ocean and winds in which they are sailing can be unpredictable. In many cases you don't know where the limits are until you find them. As one designer put it: 'The perfect racing design should sink on the finish line. Then you know that there is no extra strength built in.' Sadly, these days many of the yachts are breaking or sinking long before they get to the finish line and that applies to yachts that are just sailing across one ocean as well as those setting out to circumnavigate the world. In the 2008 Vendee Globe race around the world only 11 of the 30 starters completed the course, an unacceptable level of attrition.

Storms have a punishing effect on both yachts and their crews, which can be bad enough, but when you add in the pressures of racing, where the crew need to keep pushing almost to the point where something is going to break, it is small wonder that some yachts are taken beyond the point of no return. Modern communications and storm forecasting can help to route racing yachts away from extremes but the risk is always there. It is argued that these ocean yacht races put potential rescuers in danger by having to go out in storm conditions and that, because this is a leisure activity, the crews have no business exposing themselves to

As one designer put it: 'The perfect racing design should sink on the finish line.'

this sort of risk in remote corners of the world. The same criticism is never levelled at commercial ships that need rescue but are out there to make money which, it could be argued, is a less valid motive than an individual challenging himself to the limits. It has long been a tradition of the sea that seafarers will go to the aid of another in distress, whatever the circumstances, because it may be them in trouble next time. Long may this tradition continue.

There have been considerable casualties in storms in more regular racing. The Fastnet storm in 1979, when 15 yachtsmen lost their lives, shows the disastrous effect that an unforecast storm can have on a racing fleet. That particular disaster had a significant effect on the design and development of ocean racing yachts and led to a major rethink about yacht racing in open waters but still the accidents continue. The Sydney to Hobart race in Australia has a reputation of sudden and unpredictable storms and the route takes the competitors through the often-stormy waters of the Bass Strait. The worst of these races was in 1998 when massive storms swept the course and six crew members died, five boats were lost and only around half of the boats that started the race made the finish.

Fishing boats are another type of small craft that can go a long way offshore in search of fish and thus become exposed to storms with no time left to run for shelter. Even when a storm is forecast there is always the temptation to make one more haul before the conditions deteriorate to the point where hauling becomes impossible or dangerous. It can be a fine judgement for the skipper as to when this point is reached and the large list of fishing boat casualties suggests that decisions are made too late in many cases and a fishing boat often has to ride out the storm rather than run for shelter. Once again it is gear failures that often start the boat on the slope to disaster. With fishing boats operating on single engines and maybe dubious maintenance records, fishing is reckoned to be one of the most dangerous occupations around.

Even on passage, fishing boats can be at risk. On a delivery from France to the UK the fishing boat *Le Mediateur* encountered an Atlantic storm as it rounded Ushant. One of the crew takes up the story: 'We were barely making headway, with just steerage

Coping with storm conditions under power. The throttles are the key control when driving a powerboat in these extreme conditions.

SAFEHAVEN MARINE

way, when the bows rose, rose and rose some more, then with a huge crash the wave broke over the bows and cascaded down the deck. As it met the wheelhouse front it was forced up and in doing so lifted the wheelhouse windows. The wheelhouse was flooded to such an extent that we had to open the side doors to let the water out. It was blowing Force 9 with gusts to 70 knots and the big Atlantic swells needed very little wind to turn them into careering mountains of water.'

There is a growing trend for adventurous owners of motorboats to join the ocean cruising fraternity. The majority of ocean cruising under motor takes place in those ocean areas where the weather can generally be relied on to give a comfortable voyage. Motorboats can make a good passage along the trade wind routes and might even seek out those areas noted for calms such as the Doldrums and the temperate high pressure areas such as the Azores High. I have crossed the Atlantic from Gibraltar to New York in a fast motor cruiser and we experienced no more than a Force 4 wind the whole way. However, as this book demonstrates, no part of the ocean is free from storms so the risk of an encounter is always there.

The Fastnet storm in 1979, when 15 yachtsmen lost their lives, shows the disastrous effect of an unforecast storm on a racing fleet.

Provided that it is strongly built and can be battened down securely, a motorboat can, in some respects, be better off than a sailboat when a storm is approaching. Without having to rely on the wind, a motorboat has much more freedom of action than a sailboat because it can head in any desired direction, so there is more choice for avoiding action. There is not the vulnerability that can come from having to handle the sails in strong winds and there is not the mast and rigging to worry about. On the other hand, it is very unlikely that even an ocean-going motorboat will be self-righting in the event of a capsize so the option of running before a storm could be removed because this is where the boat could be most at risk of broaching and capsizing. The option of just lying a-hull may not be a good idea either because the boat could end up beam-on to the heavy breaking seas where a rollover becomes a real risk.

Just as with sailboats, there is no clear option about the best course of action for a motorboat caught out in a storm. At least a lee shore should not have the same risk because the boat can be driven upwind. There is also a limited amount of experience on which to draw about motorboats in storms but, provided the boat has adequate fuel and is strongly built, heading into or just off the waves could be the best

Waves can have an explosive impact on the hulls of boats in storm conditions.

option. In order to survive in storm seas a motorboat does need to enough headway to maintain good steerage, so that it is not knocked off course by breaking seas. You might think that this could be a good tactic for sailboats that have auxiliary engines and it is one possibility but few sailboats would have adequate fuel to keep the engine running for 24 hours or more and the auxiliary engines may not have enough power to keep the yacht head to wind.

There are tried and tested techniques for both power and sail under storm conditions. A steadying sail on a mast close to the stern can help to keep a boat head to wind and reduce the rolling whilst towing warps can help in following seas. These warps not only slow the boat down in its headlong rush downwind but the pull they exert at the stern can help the steering considerably. A drogue can have the same effect and was the established technique for motorboats in heavy following seas when negotiating the breaking seas in harbour entrances. It is quite remarkable how the drogue can give full steerage control under the breaking waves of a storm and it feels like the hand of God on the steering wheel, such is the dramatic improvement in control. However, few boats carry drogues these days and they will only work well on double-ended boats and displacement hulls. A good drogue can exert a pull of over three tons at the stern so everything needs to be very strong and it will only work if the boat is under full power.

Today the chances of yachts, both sail and power, getting caught out in storms is reduced. Those still most at risk are the racing boats, where the pressure of competition can lead to a higher level of breakage and there is a strong motive to keep going in deteriorating conditions. One of the most knife-edge types of competitive sailing is record breaking and here you are looking for strong consistent winds, which might be fine if winds were ever consistent, and you find yourself constantly trying to find that delicate balance between too much and too little wind.

Although it should be possible to avoid storms these days, some storms can be too extensive to escape. At least if you know what is going on with the weather you are in a stronger position than the sailors of old. However, there are no guarantees that you can escape the storms and any yacht, sail or power, that looks to cruise offshore must be prepared for the storm experience. A sound boat and a strong crew are the best defences and remember that you should be negotiating with the storm rather than fighting it. You will always be bargaining from a position of weakness but that is better than fighting a storm where there is every chance that the storm will win.

World Weather and Storm Creation

Global weather is a hugely complex subject and many factors come into play but there are some general patterns that set the scene. The main driving force for generating winds is differences in temperature, with hot air rising and cold air falling. The basic pattern is for the hot air to rise at the equator where it is hottest and then flow out north and south before descending when it gets to colder regions and then flow back towards the equator to fill the gap caused by the rising air. In reality, this flow of air is never true north and south because the Earth is rotating, so the flow is usually at an angle of about 45° to the north/south line. There are also significant 'wind cells' that divide up the basic flow. Rather than being a flow from the equator to the poles and back again, the basic circulation is actually divided into three main cells.

It was a long time before this pattern of airflow was discovered but the clue was in the high-pressure areas that lie in what are known as the Horse Latitudes. This is a relatively benign area from a weather point of view and is where the winds rising at the equator have cooled at they head outwards and drop back down to the surface again. In doing so they drag down the air that lies beyond as well and this sets up the next weather cell that rotates in the opposite direction. This cell ends further north or south and there is a final cell that extends to the poles.

This air circulation around the globe demonstrates how the weather has to be considered in three dimensions rather than the two-dimensional weather that we tend to imagine taking place at the surface. It is where the winds from these main weather cells mix that we find the more extreme types of weather and if one of the winds is cold and the other one warm then, watch out, the mixing of these hot and cold winds can lead to violence.

< **Satellites have given us a whole new perspective on storms around the world.**

v **The general wind circulation between the equator and the poles.**

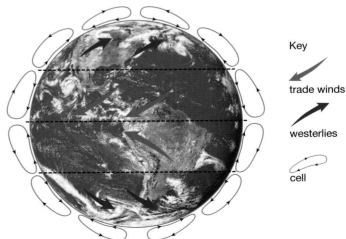

Key

trade winds

westerlies

cell

> **Trade winds blow steadily in both strength and direction and are the sailors' dream wind.**

The winds at the surface coming in from the north and the south mix around the equator but both of these winds are warm and they are rising, which is why we get the unsettled and erratic weather area known as the Doldrums. The next mixing area to the north or the south is a mainly downward flowing cold air with the surface winds moving away from each other so here the weather will tend to be on the moderate side with little in the way of extremes. The real excitement comes further to the north or the south when the two winds arrive from opposite directions: a cold wind from the north and a warm wind from the south in the Northern Hemisphere. This mixing becomes something of a battleground, with the warm air providing the energy and the cold air providing the contrast. These two opposing winds fight for supremacy and inevitably their mixing starts off a rotating wind pattern and here you have the beginnings of the run of depressions that flow from west to east across this battleground of the air. The battle lines will move north or south according to the seasons but they rarely disappear and this region is one of the world's major storm areas, usually located between 40° and 60° north and south.

Towards the equator things are less active and more predictable, with regular winds. This flow of air can be seen in the trade winds that blow steadily in both strength and direction and are the sailors' dream wind because of their consistency and predictability. If only all the winds around the world blew in this consistent manner we would probably still be using sailing ships for trade.

The trade winds tend to flow outward from the high-pressure areas that exist in temperate latitudes, which used to be known as the variables of Cancer and Capricorn. The winds also flow to the north and south of these high-pressure areas into the unpredictable and stormy wind areas between 40° and 60° north and south. Even here things might be reasonably predictable and less stormy if it was not for all the land masses that interrupt and alter the regular airflow and add to the confusion in the atmosphere. These land masses heat up much more quickly than the sea under the influence of the sun and this starts to set up more local airflows that complicate the picture. This complication is increased because the general flow to the north or south comes up against the air flowing in the opposite direction from the cold polar regions.

There is a pattern to the winds around the globe (epitomized by the trade winds) but within this general flow there is so much confusion and complexity that the situation can change from hour to hour, generally the further you go from the equator. Even in the generally predictable trade wind areas you can find tropical revolving storms that represent some of the fiercest weather on the planet and it can become easy to see why weather forecasters have more grey hairs than most. Even with their powerful computers it can still be a challenge to predict what the winds will do.

Once again the picture is complicated by other factors. The regular wind-flows around the world impart some of their energy to the sea surface to make it flow in the same direction. These major sea currents, such as the Gulf Stream and the equatorial currents, move warm water around the globe and can cause significant changes in the weather patterns because of the heat differences they generate. This water flow is just as complex as the airflow but it takes place at a slower pace.

Then there is the jet stream, an amazing very fast flowing river of air way up above 30,000 feet (9km) formed along the equatorial upper edge of the wind cells. You could be forgiven for thinking that the jet stream was just something that affected aircraft but, since the discovery of these very powerful winds back in 1945, scientists have realized that the location and speed of these rivers in the sky have a dramatic impact on what happens down at sea level. The jet stream dictates to a large degree the track and strength of the depressions that whistle across the oceans, marking as they do the line of interaction between the polar and the intermediate wind cells and, hence, the focus of strong winds.

The main jet stream is located at what might be termed the 'roll edge', at the top of the most northerly or southerly wind cell where the warm air is rising and then turning to the north or south as it cools off. Jet streams can have winds of up to 300mph, huge violent rivers of wind that can be of great benefit to high-flying aircraft but which are now thought to be the birthplace of the violent storms of the higher latitudes. The jet stream is far from being a nice steady flow of wind around the globe; its track tends to meander around and has even been known to flow north *and* south. The jet stream winds can also slow and accelerate and it is now thought that it is

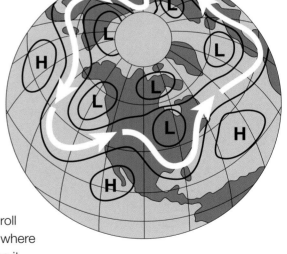

^ **The location of the jet stream at the top of the interaction between the wind cells with lows to the north and highs to the south.**

Palm trees bow to the wind in a hurricane.

these points where variations in wind speed and direction occur that are the starting points for the formation of the depressions that head across the oceans. It seems that the more we appear to understand about the weather and its formation the more we realize how much there is still to learn.

The more you look at the global weather the more you become aware of its complexity and the way that small changes in one part of the world can have a significant impact in faraway places. The only explanation for this is the Chaos Theory, that attempts to bring some sort of order out of the seeming chaos, suggesting that no change can occur in isolation so everything is interdependent. That is not a lot of help to the weather forecasters trying to make some sense out of the confusion and it is remarkable that, in view of the chaos, most of the time they get it right.

Whilst the general weather patterns around the globe help us to understand perhaps what should be happening, it is the differences in atmospheric pressure that mainly tend to dictate what is happening and will happen in the short term. This is where the synoptic chart, showing the pressures from actual readings and translated into lines of equal pressure (isobars), is so valuable. There is a direct link between the spacing of the isobar lines, the wind strength, the direction of the lines and the wind direction. Strength can be measured with a good degree of accuracy from the spacing. Wind direction is a bit more difficult because, rather than following directly along the isobar lines, it tends to spiral in towards the centre of low pressure and outward from high pressure. However, as far as storms are concerned, wind strength is what the seaman wants to know and small errors in wind direction are not so significant.

From this you might think that the forecasters have everything at their fingertips but the weather is not like that. Those isobar maps are only a general picture of what the pressure distribution is like because they are only generated from a number of spot readings, rather like joining up the lines on a graph. Those spot readings can be few and far between when it comes to areas of ocean and so, whilst they provide a guide to the patterns of wind, they do not necessarily show up the detail. It only needs those imaginary lines of pressure to move a bit closer together and there will be a stronger wind blowing. Close to land the forecasters may have a pretty good handle on the conditions but out in the ocean wind strengths can be less well defined, which accounts for the wide spread of wind strengths that may occur in a

The sails are in tatters after this yacht got caught in a storm.

forecast. Wind strengths are probably the hardest factor to define and, as we saw in the Forecasting chapter, fast moving weather systems can catch out the best of forecasters. There are so many variables in world weather that trying to forecast what is going to happen is more like intelligent guesswork than an exact science.

A forecast from this information will give wind strengths that the forecaster sees as the consistent wind strength. If only the wind behaved in this straightforward manner all would be well and you could be comfortable with a storm forecast. However, there can be many short-term variations in the wind strength with gusts that may last from a few seconds up to 10 minutes, nearly doubling the wind strength. The stronger the wind the more extreme the gusts will be and, whilst these will not have much effect on the size of the waves, they can spell disaster for sailing boats and ships, and are probably the main cause of sails blowing out.

The more you look at the wind and weather the more you realize what a hugely complex and inter-related subject this is. The world's atmosphere is one huge heat engine, with its energy generated by the sun and translated into the movements of the air around the globe. From the general flow patterns defined at the beginning of this chapter there are a multitude of eddies and alternating flows where the air masses interact with each other and with land masses, and where there are temperature differences. On a large scale these eddies can be seen in the large low-pressure areas that generate stronger winds across the northern and southern oceans. On an intermediate scale there are more local disturbances such as the tropical revolving storms, and on a very local scale there are squalls, thunderstorms and gusts that can all generate violent winds. All this is happening in three dimensions and the huge amount of energy involved can be judged by the fact that just one thunderstorm can hold the power of a nuclear explosion. The sailor attempts to harness these often-violent winds and tries to negotiate with them in order to make progress across the oceans but we are a long way from controlling this vast powerhouse of the weather. All we can do is hope we get the forecasts right. For the sailor, storms, are a fact of life, a ruling force that can still, after hundreds of years of experience, dictate whether he reaches harbour safely or whether his life hangs in the balance.

Wind strengths can vary wildly in storm conditions.

Tropical
Revolving
Storms

Tropical revolving storms are the most violent storms found at sea with winds of up to 150 knots or more. They are the pinnacle of the storm experience and these extreme storms go under various names in different parts of the world. In the Atlantic they are called hurricanes, in the west Pacific they are typhoons and in the Indian Ocean and Australia they are cyclones. From this you can see that these storms occur quite widely around the world and, while it is their destructive impact when they hit land that grabs the headlines, they spend most of their active life over the sea and they present a real hazard to shipping.

As far as the Western world is concerned, hurricanes were discovered by Christopher Columbus as a by-product of his discovery of America. His various landfalls in the Caribbean must have taken him right into the path of the Atlantic hurricanes although it is reported that he was on land when he had his first hurricane experience. Although coming from Europe, where strong winds can sweep in from the Atlantic, the winds of a hurricane must have been an exceptional experience. Hurricane wind-strengths can be double those of regular Atlantic storms and their destructive force must have been terrifying. Long before this the Chinese and Japanese were aware of the force of the typhoons, and in India the cyclones sweeping into the Bay of Bengal would have been at least annual events. Storms of this strength would have been looked on as the wrath of God or whatever deity was in favour and the effect and destruction on land tends to be recorded. Columbus was the first seaman to go on record about hurricane phenomena.

For centuries the violent winds of these revolving storms were a hazard to trade and countless ships must have been overwhelmed by their power. In the Atlantic, hurricanes form in the trade wind belt that was the favoured route for shipping heading to the New World from Africa or the Mediterranean. Without the benefit of modern-day forecasting a ship would get little warning of an approaching storm and little time to take avoiding action even if the captain could guess the path of the storm. A hurricane would approach from astern, travelling at perhaps twice the speed of the ship under sail running before the trade wind breezes. The high cloud of the hurricane and perhaps a growing swell would be the first warning signs, maybe giving 10 hours' notice of the approaching storm. If the hurricane

Tracks of tropical storms recorded on a worldwide basis.

was approaching from dead astern would it be best to bear away to the north or south? With hindsight we now know that the best course of action in the Northern Hemisphere would be to turn to the south, because most hurricanes tend to veer towards the north in their track across the ocean but the one thing we have learnt in trying to predict the path of hurricanes is their unpredictability.

As commerce expanded, those early trading ships would have encountered the cyclones of the Indian Ocean. In the Atlantic the hurricanes form north of the equator but in the Indian Ocean they can form both north and south of this line and they will then tend to travel further north or south as they progress so there would have been a greater chance of encountering tropical revolving storm here. At the western side of the Pacific there is a similar pattern for the typhoon paths, heading both north and south of the equator so that the coasts of China and Japan come into the firing line as well as those of Indonesia and Australia. On the east side of the Pacific there are hurricanes that do not conform to the regular pattern and these infrequent storms tend to head away from land to be lost in the vastness of the Pacific Ocean.

Because of the destructive power of these tropical revolving storms there has been a tremendous amount of research put into discovering the first signs of a developing storm, tracking the storm along its ocean path and then forecasting where it will go and when and where it will strike land. Much of the focus is on the latter aspect because, unlike shipping, the land cannot move out of the way so the only remedy is enough warning to secure everything or to evacuate. As far as shipping and yachts are concerned, the tracking of the storms in the present day should give enough advanced warning for even the slowest sailing yachts to take avoiding action. Today there is really no excuse for being caught out in these storms unless, of course, radio communications have been lost or do not exist and then you have to revert back to reading the weather signs.

Tropical revolving storms have caused havoc amongst shipping since earliest times but the impetus for tracking them and for predicting their future paths came during the Second World War, when naval activities

> **Dramatic clouds are part of a tropical storm but it is the winds that are the real danger.**

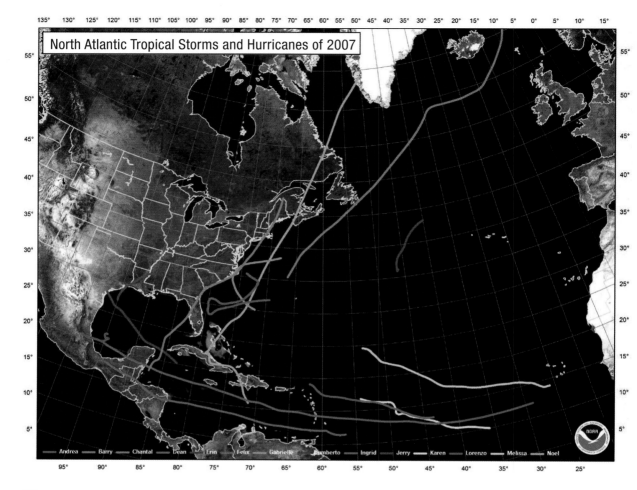

North Atlantic Tropical Storms and Hurricanes of 2007

Andrea — Barry — Chantal — Dean — Erin — Felix — Gabrielle — Humberto — Ingrid — Jerry — Karen — Lorenzo — Melissa — Noel

The hurricane tracks for a single year, showing just how difficult it can be to forecast where a hurricane is going.

in the Pacific became vulnerable to typhoons. This provided the incentive for the storm warning centre to be set up at Guam. Ironically, this warning centre was destroyed in a typhoon in 1962 and is now located at Pearl Harbor. In the US the Hurricane Warning Center is based in Miami in Florida, and Japan also has its own centre. The storms are seasonal and the early tracking systems used aircraft to fly out at high altitude and get visual pictures of the weather activity below. Tropical storms have a very distinctive appearance when seen from above, with their rotating mass of cloud and the clear centre or 'eye'. Once detected by aircraft it was a relatively simple matter to keep track of the storm but the forecasters wanted more. Knowing where a storm is located is one thing but forecasting where it is going is another and even today, with a lot of historical data for reference and with the benefit of virtually continuous satellite tracking, the vital forecasting of the future path of the storm, and the time and place of its landfall, is still an uncertain science. It seems that no two tropical storms follow the same track so every one is a new experience for the forecasters.

Over the years certain rules have been developed about the formation and behaviour of tropical storms. They cannot form within about 8° of the equator because they need the Earth's Coriolis effect to get them rotating. This Coriolis effect is created by the Earth spinning on its axis and it means that the wind direction is deflected at an angle. Then, because the energy required by the storm comes from heat, the temperature of the seawater has to be over 28°C, so that reduces the number of possible formation locations. The storm is started by one or more thunderstorms formed by hot air rising over the sea and in its early stage a tropical storm is little more than an overgrown thunderstorm with a rotating format. However, the airflow in a thunderstorm is generally up and down and it is only when these moving air masses start to spin that the storm is transformed into a revolving storm. Even then it can die away unless it is fed more heat energy from the sea – not all the embryo storms that form over the sea reach maturity and set out on their destructive paths. Those that do always head in a westerly direction, although in their later stages and when they are further north in the Northern Hemisphere they can switch to a northerly or north-easterly heading. A long path over warm seas can feed the storm with energy but once over land the strength can decay because it is not picking up more energy. If the storm passes over land and then reaches the sea again it may pick up strength and continue. You can see this with some of the Caribbean hurricanes that cross Central America and head into the Pacific. Decay almost always takes place over land although some storms head north and decay only slowly as they lose energy when passing over cooler water. Then they can turn into extra-tropical storms or curve and join the regular procession of depressions across the higher latitudes.

It can take from three to five days for tropical storms to reach maturity and they tend to last for seven to ten days. However, like most things associated with storms, there is no certainty about the track, the speed and the life of a tropical storm. Most will follow curving tracks to the north or the south but storm trackers have identified 12 basic types of track that can include the storms looping back on themselves and having significant wiggles. However, there are certain rules that these

In 1944 a typhoon east of the Philippines was responsible for the worst naval disaster in US history with the loss of 790 lives.

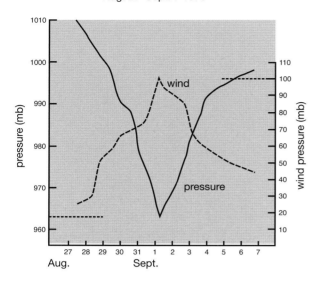

Hurricane Frances
Aug. 27–Sept. 7 1976

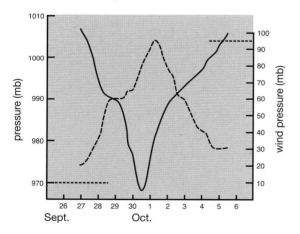

Hurricane Gloria
Sept. 26–Oct. 5 1976

As the pressure drops inside a hurricane the wind speed increases.

storms obey; they will head in a generally westerly direction on the initial track and they will always curve away from the equator. The various storm warning centres then try to guess the path of a storm. With experience and much detailed information about the storm and its surrounding weather patterns, in most cases they get it right in time to give ships and yachts adequate warning.

The structure of a tropical storm is quite fascinating and changes very little from storm to storm. It is always the eye of the storm that holds the attention, an oasis of delusionary calm in the midst of a wild storm. The eye might offer a brief respite from the violence of the storm but if you are in there you know there is going to be worse to come. Advice on how to cope with a storm divides the storm into two halves: the dangerous semicircle and the navigable semicircle. A ship can tell which semicircle she is in by the way the wind is changing. In the dangerous semicircle the wind will veer (turn clockwise) and in the navigable one it will back (anticlockwise). If the wind remains steady in direction the chances are the ship is directly in the path of the storm. With this information, a ship in the dangerous semicircle should alter course to starboard to try to get out of the storm or to port if she is in the other semicircle. These rules apply to the Northern Hemisphere and the opposite action would be required in the Southern Hemisphere. The dangerous semicircle is so-called because that side of the storm is in the northerly direction towards which the storm may curve in the Northern Hemisphere and being there could lead the ship into the eye of the storm as it curves and prolong the storm agony.

You can imagine, before storm plotting and forecasts could be sent by radio, that a ship caught up in a storm had to work out its own salvation. A book written in 1876 called *The Law of Storms Considered Practically* tries to set out the actions to be taken in storms and relates the practical experiences of ships caught in these storms. At that time research into storms was still in its infancy because, both on land and at sea, observers were more concerned with survival than keeping a plot of what was happening. It took a long time before it was realized that these violent storms were actually rotating. Today we have much more detailed knowledge of these storms and, as they are tracked and forecast with considerable accuracy, as far as shipping is concerned they have lost some of their fear and dread.

In 60 years at sea I have experienced two hurricanes, one at sea and one in port, and, given the choice, I would rather be at sea. The one at sea was in the Pacific on the west side of Central America. We were in a 6,000 ton ship and had little warning of the approach of the storm as storm tracking in this area had not been highly developed at that time as the storms were moving away from land. The wind had been increasing all day and we had been easing the speed to cope with the increasing size of the waves but keeping it high enough to maintain steerage way. The visibility was close to zero so it was difficult to judge the scale of the seas but we knew they were big when one wave climbed on board and smashed the lifeboats on the port side. For 24 hours the ship was battered by the storm. The noise was incredible, with the screaming of the wind and the crashing of the waves and the ship was a mess when it came out of the storm with even the steel plate that protected the galley entrance ripped away by the waves. You say a silent prayer that the engine will keep going because a failure there will put the ship totally at the mercy of the storm. It is the sheer elemental power of the wind and seas that dominates everything and you emerge on the other side feeling battered and mentally bruised.

A modern fast lifeboat designed to combine high speed with all-weather capability.

The hurricane in harbour was scary, not so much because of the strength of the wind but because of the debris that was flying about. We were tied up to a rather rickety wooden jetty in Cuba and when the storm was forecast the jetty looked as if it might give way under the violence of the storm. To reduce the strain on the mooring ropes the ship's holds were flooded and the ballast tanks filled so that the ship sat on the seabed and we rode out the storm that way. The air was full of sheets of corrugated iron, bits of tree and other debris and to go outside was to risk your life. We could have gone to sea to avoid this but that would have left us still close to land when the storm hit and the one thing you want in a hurricane is plenty of sea room.

The size of waves in tropical storms may not be as large as might be expected considering the strength of the winds. Firstly, the wind does not have the long fetch, the distance over which it is blowing, for the wave size to develop to full maturity and, secondly, the sheer strength of the wind tends to blow the tops off the waves, reducing their height. However, there is conflicting evidence about wave heights, some suggesting modest waves and some suggesting extreme waves. For instance, a series of observations of wave heights in US hurricanes showed wave heights in the region of 40ft (12m), which are significant but nothing extreme. In contrast, the US Navy had seabed wave gauges installed in the path of the Category 4 hurricane Ivan in the Gulf of Mexico in 2005 that recorded wave heights of over 90ft (27m) with the average wave height of 60ft (18m). I find it quite easy to believe that there must be some extreme waves within the turbulence of a tropical storm, if only because the winds are generating wave patterns that travel in different directions in different parts of the storm. Where these wave trains interact there must be some extreme transient wave peaks that could be double the average wave height or more.

Many sailing ships must have been lost in tropical revolving storms in the past but when a ship without radio is lost there is no record. Modern ships should be able to ride out the storm provided they suffer no structural damage. It was a weakened hull that is thought to have destroyed the bulk carrier Derbyshire when she encountered a typhoon in the China Sea. She disappeared with all hands. Ships should be built strong enough to cope with hurricane winds and sea but they can be vulnerable in other ways, for instance water going down the funnel or hatch covers breaking in the extreme conditions. Anything that could lead to failure of the engines or steering in these extreme conditions makes the ship vulnerable. The crews of ships are inside, protected from the extreme winds and their effect on the human body, so there is not so much risk here unless they have to go on deck to fix something. For yacht crews it is a different story and John Caldwell describes his experience of having to go out on deck when caught in a hurricane north of the Cook Islands in the Pacific:

'I was lying flat on the deck and the prying fingers of the wind caught the loose fold in my shirt, tearing away the buttons and ripping it down the back until it lay in tatters. I didn't dare try to stand or even sit and when I looked into the wind I felt my eyeballs depress. I could feel my hair whip against my cheeks.'

After completing his task he made the mistake of trying to sit up. 'An explosive wind bent me at a helpless angle and I was washed

The sort of conditions that you might find inside a tropical storm, but in reality photographs are impossible.

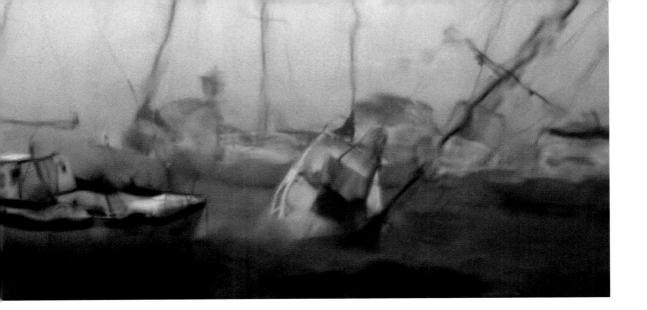

overboard but fortunately the lifeline held and I managed to reboard.' Caldwell recalls when his 29ft (8.8m) yacht entered the eye of the storm. 'Her pitching and rolling became suddenly beyond what I had ever felt before. She pitched so high that it seemed incredible that her keel was not jerked off. Great pyramids of water bolted mast-high from the sea surface.' That last comment suggests the sort of clapotic sea that would be expected in the eye of a storm but to get there is only half the story. To escape the hurricane you need to go right through the other side.

The sheer violence of the movement of the yacht is extremely debilitating and one suggestion from an experienced yachtsman after being caught out in a hurricane is: 'Stow all sail, make sure every loose item is stowed and lash yourself in your bunk until the storm is over. You won't be able to sleep because of the extreme noise of the wind and waves and the creaking and movement of the yacht but with luck the yacht and its crew will survive.'

Tropical storms dominate the headlines when they occur and there is no denying their destructive force. On land they can have a very violent impact and cause enormous damage. Any particular land area at risk from these storms may only experience them every five years or so and many do not have the full violence of a Category 5 storm, the maximum on the storm warning scale, where winds can reach 200 knots. At sea ships and yachts should get adequate warning about the location and forecast track of a storm in time to take avoiding action, so much of the threat of these storms has gone, but it will never disappear completely because, like everything to do with the weather, nothing about storms is certain.

Extreme Waves

For hundreds of years sailors have returned to harbour with tales of huge waves overwhelming their vessels. They may be called rogue or freak waves but these are really extreme waves, something way out of the ordinary as far as the regular pattern of waves in concerned. These extreme waves have often been considered to be folklore, the product of imaginative sailors' minds. Then authoritative reports emerged, followed by some dramatic photos and the world of extreme waves became reality. Today there is sophisticated wave measuring technology and satellite observations to help detect these waves and the world is waking up to the fact than the conditions out in the oceans are much wilder than was thought. The 100ft (30m) wave that was thought to be the product of science fiction has now been measured and is a reality. For the sailor, the thought of such waves is a daunting prospect and these extreme waves are much more frequent occurrences than previously thought.

Although there are no definitions about the terms, my feeling is that any wave that is over 70ft (20m) in height is an extreme wave and waves on this scale can be divided into two types. There are the transient extreme waves, those that make a temporary appearance and then disappear, and those that form part of a wave train and exist for some period of time. Apart from their lifespans, one of the main differences between these two types of extreme wave is that it is more difficult to forecast the appearance of transient waves but those that form part of a more continuous wave train should be predictable. The science of extreme waves is still in its infancy in terms of how they are formed, how they can be forecast and how we can cope with them. The need to understand these extremes is vital for the offshore oil industry, where platforms tend to be built to cope with the '100 year wave', a wave that is predicted to occur once every 100 years. Evidence is suggesting that these are occurring much more frequently, leading to a revision of the criteria used to design platforms. Those extreme waves are lurking out there and, whether they are transient or longer-lasting, they present a considerable threat to both shipping and structures fixed to the seabed.

Extreme waves can arrive with very little warning.

▽ An oil rig that was damaged by extreme sea conditions.

While there is a growing body of evidence about the existence of extreme waves and their increasing size there is no doubt about the statistics. Figures from the British National Institute of Oceanography calculated using a random process formula suggest that if you take the average height of waves in a wave train then one wave in 23 will be twice the average height and one wave in 1,175 will be three times the average height. Those figures will give seamen pause for thought but the additional chilling statistic is that one wave in

300,000 will be four times the average height. Think about that and you have the prospect of meeting a massive 66ft (20m) wave when the average wave height is just 16ft (5m)! However, to put this into perspective, 300,000 waves is an awful lot of waves, one wave every 6,000 miles or so. Those statistics also only refer to one spot so if you move around you could miss the big waves altogether. It is fixed stations such as oil platforms that should be more concerned by these statistics. In one major hurricane in the Gulf of Mexico a number of oil platforms were damaged by wave impact on the underneath of the platform deck. This is the area of the platform that is designed to be clear of the water at all times except possibly with that 100 year wave.

These extreme waves are only the highest in relation to their particular sea state and the average height to which they relate could be quite small, maybe in the region of 3ft (1m) for the larger waves in the series. Such mini-extreme waves could pass almost unnoticed and be seen as little more than the wash of a passing ship. In my 60 years at sea I have only come across two extreme waves that caused concern. One was when we were searching for a fisherman who was reported washed off the rocks. We were in a lifeboat looking just outside the surf line where a big sea was breaking in a north-westerly onshore gale. We would have gone inside the surf if we had seen someone to rescue but the risk was too great while we were only searching. As you can imagine, all eyes were turned towards the shore to look for the man in the water and then suddenly I was conscious of it going dark. I looked to seaward and there was a monster wave rearing up alongside us with the sun shining weakly through it. You know when the sun is shining through a wave that you don't want to be on the lee side of it and it looked as if this nearly vertical wall of water was going to curl over and crash over us. It was too late to do anything but pray and we went up the side of that wave like an express elevator and toppled over the crest just as the wave broke. That wave must have been three or four times the average wave height and it was breaking in deeper water. We had a narrow escape and it brought home to me that there are always big ones out there and you need to allow margins for them.

The second extreme wave was to the north of Iceland during the Cod War. I was on a very large ocean-going tug and our job was to protect the fishing fleet from the Icelandic gunboats. The tug was running before the big seas at slow speed and I remember watching big waves curling up behind us and then passing under the ship. Then a monster reared up its ugly head like a vertical wall of water with the crest breaking. It must have been 40–50ft (12–15m) high, several times higher than the regular waves, and it crashed over the stern and swept over much of the forward superstructure. The seas off Iceland in the winter are not my favourite place and I got the feeling that that wave was trying to tell us something.

I have mentioned the two types of extreme waves and it is the transient type that can be the more frightening and damaging. It is thought that these are caused by two phenomena and the really bad ones could be a combination of the two. Firstly, waves very rarely come in just one clean and tidy wave train with all the waves spread evenly and heading in the same direction. That could happen in an ideal world but in the real world there may be two or more wave trains in the same part of the ocean. There can be waves generated by the prevailing wind and there can be decaying waves remaining from a preceding storm or generated quite recently by the same storm heading in a different direction because the wind has changed. Look closely at the sea and you can pick out different wave trains – it is when the crest of two or more of these waves meet that the wave height can be increased dramatically. When wave crests meet, the height of each individual wave is added to the total so three 13ft (4m) wave crests could produce a 39ft (12m) transient wave peak. It is transient because the height will drop as soon as one or more waves passes on but if you happen to be in that spot at that time you will experience a dramatic wave peak.

Then you can add into the mix the effects of currents or tides. If the waves are running against the current the wavelength will shorten and the waves will become steeper and often higher. This can generate some very nasty sea conditions with a succession of breaking crests. If this current factor combines with one of the transient wave crests then look out. You can get the same effect when waves approach shallow water. Once again the progress of the waves is slowed and they become steeper, higher and more prone to breaking. In extreme cases, where a current is travelling at a quarter of the speed of approaching waves, the waves can be stopped in their tracks and a mighty wall of water can build up that could prove fatal to small craft and dangerous to big ships. One of the earliest

reports of a ship being lost to an extreme wave occurred in 1909 when the steamer *Waratah* disappeared along with all her passengers and crew after leaving Durban heading for Cape Town, following the route of the notorious Agulhas Current.

The other type of extreme wave can occur when there is a very long fetch; winds that are blowing in the same direction over 1,000 miles or more of ocean. Whilst the waves generated by these winds should be regular, it is thought that there can be a resonance in some waves that makes them travel faster than others so these waves will overtake and cause extreme waves.

There is an increasing interest in these waves, which has led to research into the phenomenon. One thing the research has thrown up is that extreme waves occur with a much greater frequency than was previously thought, but this is not hard to appreciate when you

Even in inshore waters, there is still a danger of extreme waves.

SAFEHAVEN MARINE

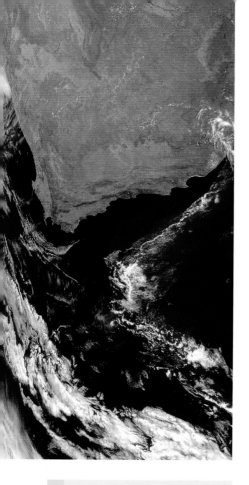

A satellite image of Cape Agulhas, where extreme waves are a familiar hazard.

consider that as recently as the 1980s the detection of these waves relied entirely on ships sighting or experiencing them. A ship has to be in the vicinity of a wave for it to be detected and at night the wave might not be seen or its size appreciated. Today there are more sophisticated means of detecting extreme waves, such as radar scanning and satellite detection. Radar is used mainly from fixed platforms to detect and measure the wave heights around the platform and is used mainly to gather data from offshore oil platforms. Satellite detection can scan much larger areas of the sea and it is largely this satellite detection that has led to the increased knowledge of frequency of extreme waves.

Under a programme known as MaxWave, funded by the EEC, a programme of satellite detection of these waves has shown that not only do the waves occur more frequently than was previously thought but they occur in most sea regions. Previously it was thought that extreme waves were only found in suspect areas such as off South Africa in the Agulhas Current, where the current combines with strong winds. However, the increased detection frequency could be because any wave just twice the significant wave height has been used in a revised specification for what constitutes an extreme wave. Any seaman will tell you from experience that waves of this size are relatively frequent experiences and the statistics given above show this. Extreme waves are what the name suggests, waves that are extreme in size and therefore much larger than the more regular waves.

Reported encounters with extreme waves have been relatively rare, although the MaxWave programme suggests that more than 200 large ships have been lost to rough seas and severe weather in the 1990s and 2000s. Whether this is due just to rough seas and damage or mechanical failure is not specified and the actual recorded encounters with extreme waves is much lower. Weather ships that have been cruising in open ocean waters on a continuous basis in the north Atlantic have recorded big waves, up to 75ft (23m) in height, and you might expect that if these extreme waves were a frequent occurrence then these weather ships would also have experienced them frequently. One instance of a weather ship meeting a recorded 90ft (27m) wave was in 2001 and this was one of the largest open ocean waves ever measured.

The officer on watch, Jan Erik Taule, described how it was that the 177ft (54m) long MV *Polar Front* encountered a 27m wave in position N 065° 55' E 002° 03'. For a couple of days the wind had been steadily WSW at gale force. On 10 November the wind increased to storm Force 10 and then to hurricane force, 56 knots with gusts to 75 knots. At midnight on 11 November he relieved the captain, Børge Misje, and was briefed on the weather conditions, especially the wave height, 59–72ft (18–22m). The ship's log recorded the wind at 55 knots from the west at midnight with snow and showery weather. In spite of the showery weather conditions it was a bright night owing to the moonlight between the showers.

'I was sitting in the chair, having my coffee, when suddenly I saw a heavy sea rising in front of the ship, some distance away, and knew that this would be a nasty one. It looked quite scary in the moonlight with a lot of foam on top of the wave. I switched from autopilot to manual steering and at the same time gave more engine power, trying to meet the monster dead ahead. Luckily I managed to do so and the wave lifted the ship's bow in an abnormal angle. I felt that the vessel might have a problem climbing the wave and gave full ahead. The vessel climbed slowly and suddenly the air was filled with a roaring noise and the air was only foam all around. The ship shook and vibrated a lot when the propeller left the water at the top of the wave. I was standing and grabbed the steering wheel, afraid of falling. "Damn it" was the only thing I could say when the ship was over the top and started falling down the other side of the wave. I felt myself hanging in the air and could hardly remain on my feet when the ship's bow crashed into the next wall of water. The force was unlike anything I had ever felt. The seawater smashed into the front of the vessel and found its way into the accommodation through different air outlets. There was no damage to the vessel itself but in cabins, galley and other areas, furniture and loose parts were in a mess. The crew took the incident calmly – just another nasty bastard.'

This 90-footer was measured by a wave height recorder on board the *Polar Front.* A similar device was fitted to the *Research Ship Discovery* when she encountered the first 100ft (30m) wave ever recorded from a ship. Dr Penny Holliday was on board at the time and recounts the experience:

'I wasn't asleep – no chance of that when your bunk appears to be trying to throw you out of it. I was trying to stay wedged into it, with

> **'I was sitting in the chair, having my coffee, when suddenly I saw a heavy sea rising in front of the ship, some distance away, and knew that this would be a nasty one.'**

my lifejacket stuffed under one edge of my mattress, and feet jammed against the wooden sides at the bottom. But there was no sleep. It was very noisy as you can imagine. As well as the sound of wind, and the sea crashing onto the side of the ship and swishing down the decks, I could hear general banging and crashing all around. The ship creaks and groans and as it flexes the fittings make a kind of he-he-he noise which in the middle-of-the-night-paranoia sounds like your wardrobe is laughing at you! At some point the chair in my cabin flew across from its position under the desk (where I thought I had carefully wedged it tight), bounced on the floor and jumped on top of me. So some of the time I was trying to sleep, and some of the time I was just lying awake hoping things would improve. Normally on a no-work-bad-weather-night I might wander up to the bridge to chat to whoever was on watch, but with the master, the chief engineer, two lookouts and the usual bridge officers up there, us scientists could tell that it wasn't a time for a social visit.

'I couldn't honestly say I felt the biggest wave and knew what had happened, but during that night we had 23 waves that were over 20m, and I certainly could tell that this was no ordinary storm. I've been through some very bad weather several times before in the Rockall Trough and in the Iceland Basin – my worst previous being in 1996 when we had significant wave height of about 13m south of Iceland. But the violence of the motion and the obvious very deep concern of the captain, engineers and bridge officers was something I certainly hadn't known before. A particularly alarming event happened the night after the biggest waves, when the storm was still raging but the waves had decreased a little. During the night, the starboard lifeboat came loose after a roll of about 35°, and was banging against the side of the ship. The noise of each bang was tremendous – somehow made worse by it being about 4am. Some extremely brave crew were dispatched to secure it until daylight and calmer seas. In many ways, this was the most frightening thing for me to see – the bosun and ABs having to go out into that weather to do a very dangerous job. I think that was when the seriousness of our situation was brought home to me. Wanting to keep out of the

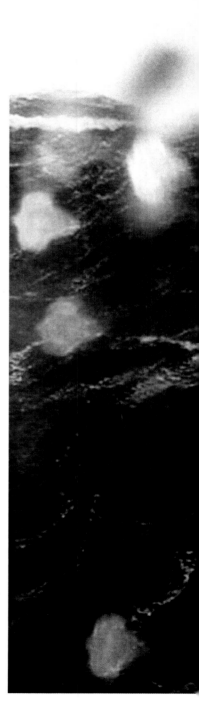

> **Not the extreme 90-footer (27m) but the view of a big wave from the bridge of the *Polar Front*.**

The view from the bridge of the Research Ship *Discovery* in a normal gale. In the 100-footer (30m) the whole front of the ship would have disappeared.

way, I stayed in my bunk, listening as the men, with harnesses and equipment clinking, opened the watertight doors outside my cabin. I think I held my breath for most of the time they were out there. But they did the job and came back.'

The *Discovery* was operating in the Rockall Trench, an area of deep water that lies between Iceland and Shetland. On the night in question the weather map showed the isobars lying west to east almost right across the Atlantic in a straight line. This created a fetch of over 1,000 miles for the waves to develop and the wave recordings were showing consistent waves of over 60ft (18m) with the winds blowing at around 50 knots. These are bad though not extreme conditions, but the crew of the ship reported that they were experiencing violent seas. The huge 100ft (30m) waves are thought to have developed in front of an active front that was traversing the area and the theory is that the extreme waves measured were created by resonance from this frontal system, focusing and boosting the energy of the waves to create the monsters that were measured.

Most of the weather ships have now been replaced by recording buoys, which are equipped with weather monitoring equipment and can send in continuous reports of weather and sea conditions. During some of the major storms that have occurred off the coast of North America these buoys are reported as having recorded waves of over 25 metres, which is over 80 feet, and because these waves are associated with violent storm conditions it is thought that they are transient peaks created in the confused seas. The buoys tend to be moored in relatively shallow waters and this is likely to increase the height of the waves compared with those in the open ocean.

What is interesting about the recording of that 100-foot wave is that the trough is deeper below the median line than the wave crest is above it. We always talk about wave height – the distance between trough and crest – and you picture a ship trying to climb over the huge crest of an extreme wave. In reality the chances are that it is the deep trough that comes either before or after the high crest that does the damage. These deep troughs or 'holes' are like the reverse of an extreme wave and when a ship or boat falls into them the chances of climbing out unscathed are small. This is when the ship is vulnerable and the following wave can deposit tons of active water on the deck to

Sections of the wave recorder on board *Discovery* showing three very big waves over a 24 hour period. The middle one is the highest ever recorded by a ship.

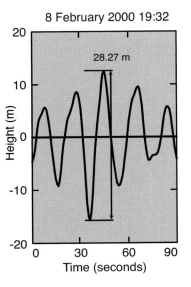

8 February 2000 19:32

28.27 m

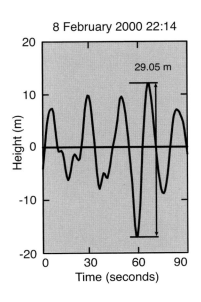

8 February 2000 22:14

29.05 m

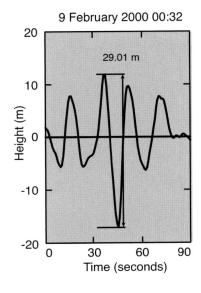

9 February 2000 00:32

29.01 m

cause serious damage. This is what happened to the *Polar Front*. There is a possibility that you might see an extreme wave crest some way off, giving you a chance to do something about it. But you don't see the hole until you fall into it and by then it is too late.

These holes exist in many types of sea conditions and there are many tales of ships and boats being affected by them. I found one in the dangerous Portland Race off the south coast of England when I was testing lifeboats. This race is notorious for its waves with wild breaking crests so it seemed a good place to see how the lifeboat would handle it. We went over the first breaking crest quite happily and then there was a hole on the other side. The whole boat became airborne and dropped into the hole where I swear you could almost see the seabed. Then the next wave fell on top of us. I was so grateful we were in a strong boat and we eventually rose clear with only superficial damage but the scary part of that hole encounter was the total lack of warning.

A similar thing is reported from ships that have experienced the wild seas off the coast of South Africa when heading south-west into a serious gale. Reports say that the ship comes over a wave crest and then just keeps going down and down. The stresses on the hull of the ship are enormous, the buoyancy trying to lift the ship and the weight of water on deck pressing it down. In many cases the stress has been too much and serious damage or sinking has been the result.

Encountering any type of extreme wave at sea is likely to be a memorable experience, assuming the vessel survives.

As we start to get a better picture of these waves and holes there are three main types of extreme waves that are emerging. There is the three sisters type where the wave is one of three very large waves and it is suggested that these are created by a secondary wave train being superimposed on the more regular waves. This may be the type of wave that the *Discovery* experienced. Then there is the wave tower, a sort of pyramid wave that exists as a single peak and could be caused in part by current focusing that causes large wave trains to cross each other at a shallow angle. Finally there is the white wall, a huge wall of water approaching that looks vertical with the crest starting to break. Several yachts and ships have reported this type of extreme wave and it must be one of the most frightening experiences of a life at sea.

Encountering any type of extreme wave at sea is likely to be a memorable experience, assuming the vessel survives. We hear the tales of survivors but how many ships and yachts have succumbed to these monsters of the deep? The *Derbyshire* was a very large bulk carrier that disappeared off the radar in a typhoon in the China Sea and examination of the wreck on the seabed showed that she had suffered a major hull fracture. The *München* was a large modern ship designed in 1978 and she disappeared without warning in an Atlantic storm. There are many more stories of recent ships being damaged in storm conditions and you have to ask how this can happen with modern technology and design.

There are two factors that seem to point to the cause. One is that many of the ships involved have had their bridge fronts well forward on the hull. Most passenger ships are built this way and the *München* followed this design style. It is not difficult to see what happens to these ships if they encounter an extreme wave with a mass of water coming over the bow and striking the vertical wall of the superstructure with incredible force. It is reckoned that the water in a major wave coming on board in this way could exert a force of 100t/sq m (9 tons/sq ft). Not many ships are built to withstand that and in the case of the *München* it could have wiped out the forward superstructure block and all the people in it. Passenger ships are regularly suffering from major wave damage and this is not new, with some major liners and cruise ships reporting wave damage at bridge level and above.

Speed is the other factor and perhaps a more worrying one as large ships get faster and have to maintain tight schedules. A modern container ship or passenger ship can be 1,000ft (300m) long and may be travelling at up to 25 knots. Because of the schedule there is no way it is going to slow down to a safe speed just in case it meets an extreme wave. Equally, at their high speed there will be no chance to slow down in time if an extreme wave is sighted ahead so they will

Extreme waves arrive with very little warning, so the helmsman always needs a reserve of speed in order to cope with the unexpected.

The nearly new 261m (856ft) cargo ship *München* disappeared without trace in 1978. It is possible that she encountered an extreme wave that swept away the bridge structure.

always be vulnerable. These large modern ships rely heavily on weather routeing to avoid the worst of the weather and that seems to work in most cases but routeing tends to rely on forecast winds rather than sea conditions. There does not seem to be any prospect of being able to forecast the existence of extreme waves in advance. In the case of the *Discovery*, the extreme waves were encountered when the wind was only blowing Force 10.

The same problem of encounters with extreme waves also applies to the growing number of fast ferries. These may be travelling at speeds in excess of 40-knots in open seas and whilst at present there are few reports of them encountering anything extreme, the possibility is always there. A 40 knot ship hitting a major wave or, perhaps worse, a deep hole, would not be good news for the ship or the passengers. Maybe the long slim monohull fast ferries might cope with an encounter with a big wave by going through it rather than over it but hitting any wall of solid water at 40 knots in any sort of craft would be an interesting experience and the wave is likely to win the contest.

In the list of ship encounters with extreme waves in most cases the height of the wave has been estimated rather than measured. When a ship encounters a wave that sweeps on board over the bow it is usually the bridge front that suffers from the impact. Knowing the height of the bridge above the waterline could give some idea of the height of the wave. However, this can only be a rough guide as a wave crest crashing on board can have considerable momentum and can sweep up to exceptional heights to cause damage. Then again, the report of the wave height may well be exaggerated in the report of the encounter in order to make it sound like a rare and unusual event that could not have been foreseen. By suggesting that this was an extreme wave encounter the captain does not get into trouble for driving his ship too fast for the conditions.

However, the estimated wave heights from some of these encounters still make frightening reading. The wave that the *München* is thought to have encountered was estimated at 66ft (20m) high whilst the Atlantic liner *Queen Elizabeth* reported a 90-footer (27m) in 1943. The German liner *Bremen* was completely immobilized and in severe danger of sinking after encountering an estimated 98-footer (30m) in the south Atlantic and there have been several cases where modern cruise liners have suffered damage and passenger injuries from extreme wave encounters.

Yachts and small craft seem to be more cautious about extreme waves. Many yachts have experience 50-or-60 footers (15–18m) but whether these were extreme amongst the general run of waves or whether the seas were generally very big is a matter of conjecture. A small craft would tend to ride over the crest of an extreme wave and drop down the other side without much harm and when yachtsmen talk of extremes it is usually when talking about how steep the wave was rather than its height. A vertical wall of water that denotes a wildly breaking crest is a significant risk to a yacht. Its height is not so critical.

There is no doubt about the existence of these extreme waves but in the reported encounters I think it is significant that many of them feature liners and cruise ships rather than cargo ships. Liners would normally travel at higher speeds than cargo ships and would generally have tighter schedules to keep so any encounter with an extreme wave is more likely to cause damage and therefore get reported. Many of the reported encounters have estimated wave heights and extreme waves that have actually been measured are relatively rare. With the growing number of weather buoys established out in the open ocean,

A cruise liner hits a big wave that could cause serious damage and injury on board.

particularly along the coasts of North America, there is the possibility of getting more wave height data. These have recorded wave heights in the 60 to 70ft (18–21m) range, which are big waves by any standards, but in the Perfect Storm, recalled in the famous book, the reported wave heights of 90ft (27m) were only recorded at around 65ft (20m) at the wave buoys.

That encounter by the *Discovery* is one of the few authenticated extreme wave measurements taken by a calibrated wave recorder. Other extreme wave heights, such as the 112-footer (34m) measured by the *USS Ramapo* in the north Pacific in 1933, were measured by triangulation, using the length of the ship and the height of the mast lined up with the top of the wave, a method that would have limited accuracy. It would be very helpful to further the study of extreme waves if more ships could be fitted with wave recorders of the type fitted to *Discovery* to give a better picture of just how frequent these damaging wave encounters are. However, you can sense a reluctance on the part of ship owners to co-operate in this because the wave recorder reading would show the precise height of the wave, thus leaving no room for exaggeration in the event of ship or cargo damage from a wave encounter.

It is not just extreme waves that can cause concern but also extreme swells. In 2008 there was an extreme swell event recorded in the Atlantic when a low-pressure area moved away from the Atlantic coast of the US. Over a 24 hour period this low deepened considerably as it moved north-east and then, as it weakened, it turned south-east. Then its movement stopped and the very strong winds from the north associated with this low had a long fetch. This, in turn, generated a very heavy swell moving outward from the low. The swell extended over most of the north Atlantic and in Puerto Rico, in the Caribbean, breaking swells of 30ft (9m) were recorded and later, as the swells developed, the breaking surf reached 40ft (12m) in height. Swells of this nature may, on their own, have little impact on shipping but when a monster swell crest coincides with a big storm wave you have the potential for an extreme wave situation.

> **Somewhere out there, in these rough seas, there could be a extreme wave, but there is very little chance of getting any warning.**

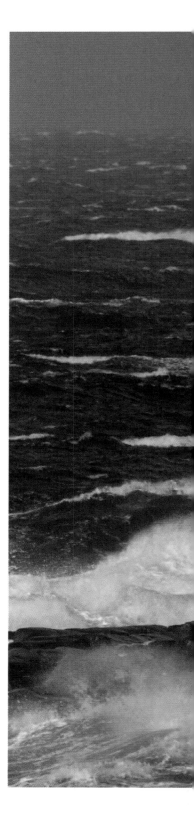

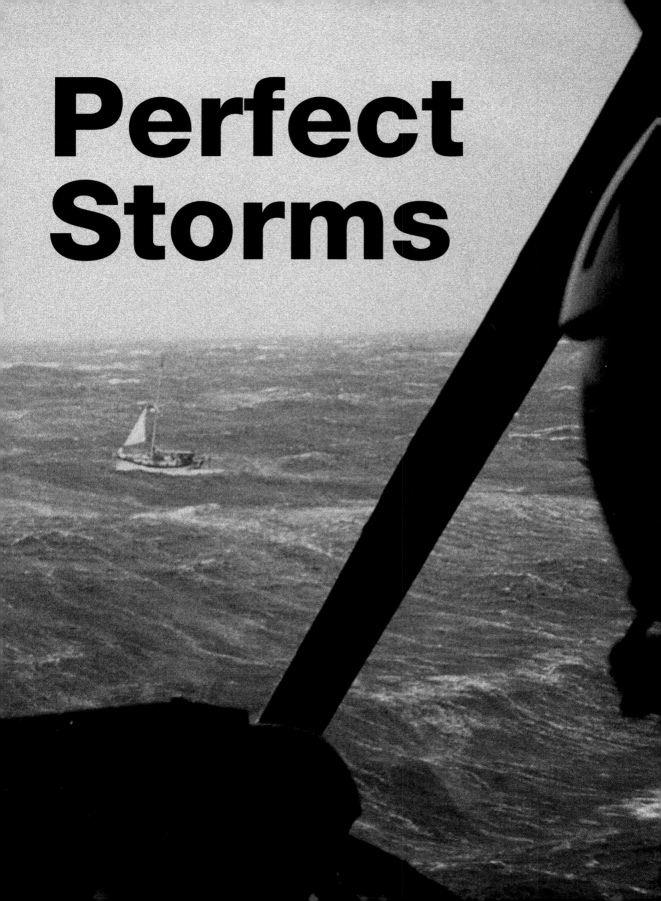

Perfect Storms

Occasionally the meteorological world goes haywire and the weather systems get totally out of step. This is when forecasting becomes a nightmare and the systems combine to create mayhem. The wind and the waves can go off the scale and, for anyone caught out at sea, life expectancy shortens quite dramatically. Fortunately, these 'perfect storms' are rare but when they happen, watch out. The normal rules for coping with bad weather do not apply.

The book *The Perfect Storm* follows the creation of just one such meteorological mishap, where the forces of nature combined to create a fight for survival for the seamen and airmen caught up in it. It is a remarkable story of what it can be like fighting for your life in conditions that are beyond the comprehension of even most seamen.

Perfect Storms tend to happen mainly in temperate climes, probably around 30 to 45° north or south of the equator, and they are usually formed from a meeting of two or more storm systems. One of these may be dying away but still have sufficient energy to vitalize and bring extra power to the system it is meeting. Certainly a vital component of a Perfect Storm is a hurricane, typhoon or cyclone that, instead of following the general trend of moving over land and dying out, has maintained a course over water and is heading away from the equator. By staying over water this tropical storm can still pick up energy from warm water which, in the case of a hurricane, will usually come from the Gulf Stream. Another cause of staying over water and heading north can be the location of a powerful cold front over the land that prevents the intrusion of the hurricane.

You have the remains of a tropical storm moving out of the tropics and steadily weakening so that the wind within the storm may have dropped to a more manageable 50 or 65 knots, still strong but some way below hurricane force. Heading north in the Northern Hemisphere, it is moving into alien territory and will usually become another low-pressure area

< **The yacht *Satori* viewed from the Coastguard helicopter.**

v **An intense low off the East Coast of North America, heading into perfect storm territory.**

that can join the procession of depressions that are a feature of the temperate latitudes. In most cases it will retain its individual identity, weakening all the time, and it will not join up with its adjoining low-pressure areas. However, if that cold front over the land on the western side of the ocean basin is very active there will be tremendous energy locked up and looking for release, perhaps first seen as a small kink in the line of the front that can gain enough impetus to start rotating. If this low meets up with the hurricane that is heading north, mayhem will result.

Like many of the more severe storms that plague the north Atlantic, the Perfect Storm of the book started with a small kink in a powerful cold front. On the weather chart a cold front looks like a nice regular straight line but, in reality, is full of activity as cold and warm air mix in often-violent fashion. On a local basis this can generate thunderstorms but when a kink forms in the front it can quickly change to a rotating motion like a mini-depression. Once the rotation has started and it picks up more energy you have the start of a full-blown depression that can have a rapidly-deepening centre and the wind strength increases immediately. In the Perfect Storm the depression started out on a course to the south-east from a point up near the Grand Banks and the violent winds enveloped the swordfish fleet that was still at sea. Further south, the tail end of a hurricane was moving north and the two storms met and amalgamated to produce the 'perfect storm'. Ships, yachts and fishing boats that were still out were caught up in the violent seas and screaming winds.

Coastguard casualties in the water waiting to be rescued during the Perfect Storm.

One of the casualties was the yacht *Satori* and it was the rescue of its crew that got Coastguard boats and helicopters into trouble. I find it amazing that the Coastguard ship *Tamaroa* even contemplated launching its RIB rescue boat in waves that were topping 60ft (18m) and winds that were off the scale. Such is the traditional heroism of rescue services around the world that it is hard to stand by and watch people die without trying to do something.

Although the book was called *The Perfect Storm* this was better known as the Halloween Storm and it caused enormous damage onshore as well as at sea. In official parlance the storm was an extra-tropical cyclone because it formed outside the tropics and picked up new energy from the warm waters of the Gulf Stream to grow to full hurricane intensity. A side effect of this storm was a huge tidal surge along the east coast of North America, creating some of the highest tides ever recorded.

On the opposite side of the world in New Zealand it was a similar set of weather circumstances that led to the loss of the passenger ship *Wahine* in 1968 when the inter-island ferry capsized in the entrance to Wellington Harbour with the loss of 53 lives. In the early hours of the morning two violent storms merged over Wellington, creating an extra-tropical storm similar to the Halloween Storm, the worst recorded storm in New Zealand's history. Cyclone Giselle came roaring down from the north and met another storm rushing up from the Antarctic. The storms collided over the Cook Strait, the narrow channel that separates the North and South Islands, and all hell was let loose.

> **I find it amazing that the Coastguard ship Tamaroa *even* contemplated launching its RIB rescue boat in waves that were topping 60ft (18m).**

It could not have happened in a worse place because the Cook Strait, even in more normal circumstances, can be a wild place. Strong winds were forecast that night but nothing like the actual intensity. The *Wahine* was used to storms, so she set out on the short crossing of the strait. Early in the morning the winds were gusting to 70 knots and the captain decided to enter Wellington Harbour. In just 20 minutes the wind had increased to 80 knots, the ship lost her radar and huge waves were knocking her off course. The captain tried to head out to sea again but he barely had control of the ship in the extreme conditions and she was driven towards Barrier Reef. The anchors were dropped to try to hold the ship but, as the winds continued to increase in strength, the ship was driven ashore. Amazingly, rescue craft were able to get to the ship in the wild conditions and rescued most of the passengers and crew before the ship capsized. Those killed were mostly the elderly and children, perhaps demonstrating that being active is a vital part of surviving a storm. It was water on the car deck that caused the ship to capsize, a story that would become familiar later with a number of Ro-Ro ship capsizes including the *Princess Victoria* and the *Herald of Free Enterprise*. That perfect storm generated the strongest winds ever recorded in New Zealand at close to 140 knots and the funnelling of the wind through the narrow Cook Strait must have had an effect on this.

The Australian north-east coast is battered by cyclones every year but one of the worst was in 1899 when the incoming cyclone met a tropical disturbance coming from the opposite direction. The result was a storm that was the most intense ever recorded in the region with 308 people losing their lives and over 100 vessels lost.

**The US coastguard cutter
Tamaroa after launching
its RIB in the Perfect
Storm.**

A perfect storm could be defined as any unusual storm that generates unpredicted conditions. People on land and at sea remember these, the ones that get talked about for years and which tend to have violence beyond normal human experience. In some cases the storms themselves might not be that extreme but for the area in which they occur. The one that hit the Fastnet fleet of yachts, causing such chaos and loss of live, could come into this category. This started as a very deep depression swinging in from the Atlantic towards Ireland but the mayhem began when the front associated with it turned across the area where many of the 300 participating yachts were racing. Not only did the passage of these fronts create a rapid increase in the wind but it also changed the wind direction, generating a confused and chaotic sea. Again, the situation was compounded when a secondary low formed to the south of the main centre and, because this did not show on the weather charts, its effects were not included in the forecast. This Fastnet Storm qualifies as a perfect storm because of its two centres and the unforecast nature of the intense winds generated.

The Channel Storm of 1956 started off as a summer depression moving in from the Atlantic towards south-west Britain, not unusual but when it encountered the land and headed up the Bristol Channel it deepened rapidly with the high ground of the Welsh mountains thwarting its passage to the north. Here was an example of the way mountains can influence the movement of storms and this one was noticeable for the violence of the winds in the English Channel, where there happened to be a yacht race in progress. The Channel experiences these perfect storms every few years. Again in 1987 the

Great Storm of that year had hurricane-force winds with a couple of yachts in trouble, caught out by the very sudden intensifying of the storm, but most of the damage was caused on land rather than at sea. This storm is remembered as the one that was not forecast, where the forecasters insisted that there was not a hurricane in the offing.

Further north in the British Isles extreme winds are reported every year or two. Some of these are caused by the remnants of hurricanes that have survived across the Atlantic and have picked up extra energy and ferocity on the way. Australia and New Zealand also have some of this type of intense storm, rare for the region, and winds have been recorded at up to 130 knots, well into hurricane territory. It is almost impossible to forecast storms of this intensity and they will probably appear in the forecast as storms with winds of 60 or 70 knots – bad enough but capable of nothing like the damage that a 130-knot storm can do.

These perfect storms are mainly found in the Northern Hemisphere because of the land masses that can change the flow of depressions. Both high land and temperature differences can bring about short-term changes in the weather patterns that are difficult or even impossible to forecast and so they fall into the category of unusual events. It is easy to sense the frustration of forecasters wanting to understand and predict them but handicapped by their unusual nature and circumstances. As a forecaster you do not get good marks for forecasting extreme events that do not materialize. In the Southern Hemisphere there are far fewer and smaller land masses to influence the air flows and weather patterns so these are free to adopt more predictable paths. The perfect storms here tend to be focused to the south of Australia and New Zealand and in the wild waters around Cape Horn, suggesting that the extremes of weather are much more likely in the vicinity of land than out in the open ocean.

The Ro-Ro ferry *Wahine* aground and listing as the crew and passengers evacuate the ship after being overwhelmed by the powerful winds.

When the Storms Meet the Land

Out in the open ocean there is a degree of regularity about storm-generated seas. While there is always the risk of extreme waves and other unexpected events, the seas are relatively predictable compared with the seas close to land. Waves need deep water to maintain their regular pattern so, once you introduce shallow water, land, tides and the twists and turns of the coastline that interfere with the normal flow of waves, chaos reigns. If you thought that open sea storm waves were bad they are nothing compared with what can occur inshore.

Inshore waters are the place where storm waves start to release some of their energy and you can see this when the waves hit the rocks in violent displays of spray. These are harmless to shipping and boats but it is a little further out, where the waves start to touch the bottom, that the impact of storm waves in the shallows is first seen and where danger lurks. Once the storm waves start to feel the seabed they are slowed down and this shortens the wavelength which, in turn, makes the waves steeper. When a wave reaches a slope angle of around 18° it is in danger of breaking at the crest and immediately it does so the danger increases for shipping and, particularly, for boats. The bigger the waves the further out to sea they will reach this critical angle so huge storm waves can present a real danger as they approach the coast.

There is often a deep and menacing swell associated with storms at sea and these waves have a long wavelength, their influence extending deeper underwater than for regular waves. As they move from deep ocean waters onto the relatively shallow continental shelf they can lead to a noticeable change in the sea conditions, a shortening of the wavelength and a greater willingness to break at the crest, combined with a steepening of the wave gradient. This effect can be seen particularly in the Bay of Biscay, where the change tends to occur around the line of the main shipping route and this has contributed to the evil reputation of the region.

These effects on storm waves can be relatively minor compared with the effects of the tides and currents that are found close to land in many parts of the world. We have seen the consequences of the Aghulas Current flowing south along the coast of South Africa

Round Island Lighthouse on the Isles of Scilly showing the explosive impact of waves from an Atlantic storm. The light is 170ft (52m) above sea level.

Breaking waves as the storm meets shallow water.

against the prevailing wind from the south-west. The same effect of a shortening of the wavelength and steeper wave gradients can be found in many coastal areas when the wind is blowing against the tide. The difference is that the tide will turn every six hours so the wind against tide effect will be cyclical, changing with the tide direction. In some areas, when the tide runs strongly the change can be quite dramatic, changing from a quite moderate and normal storm sea into a wild maelstrom of steep, dangerous waves in just an hour.

The flow of the tidal currents is very much affected by the shape of the land so the strength of the tide tends to be focussed around protruding headlands. Winds are also concentrated in a similar way by high land so that the strength of storm winds can be increased considerably around these points and through narrow channels. Add in the effects of shallow waters and you can see why shipping has always been nervous about approaching land. On the one hand the land offers the prospect of a safe harbour and shelter from the storm but on the other it presents a very real danger before that shelter can be found. Until the advent of electronic navigation the approach to land in a storm was made even more dangerous by the uncertainty about the ship's position, and the storm-force seas could restrict its ability to manœuvre and bear away from the dangers of the land. Small wonder that making a landfall was considered to be the most dangerous part of any voyage and the record of ships lost in storms close to land is long and distressing.

Before the advent of GPS satellite positioning, one of the big unknowns in navigation was leeway, the effect that strong winds might have in blowing a ship sideways off its course. In a Force 8 wind the pressure can around 5lbs/sq ft (24kg/sq m) so a high-sided cargo ship or a sailing ship could have a lateral pressure of many tons pushing it off course. My earliest rescue at sea was from a 6,000-ton cargo ship with no cargo on board and riding high in the water, blown off course in a blizzard. This was off the west coast of Scotland and we were making so much leeway that we ended up on the rocks on one of the off-lying islands. This was before electronic navigation, we were lost and it took some time for the lifeboat to find us in the zero visibility of the blizzard.

> **More lifeboats have been lost coming back into harbour with the survivors of a rescue than in the open sea trying to effect a rescue.**

The accuracy of GPS today gives confidence about the vessel's position but can result in dismissing the dangers of storm-force seas close to land. Even when a vessel arrives off a harbour the danger is not over. The harbour entrance is where a strong current running out can meet storm waves pouring in from seaward and there can be the added danger of shallow water. It all adds up to what can be the greatest danger to small craft when a storm is blowing. The temptation to get into the safety of harbour is strong yet the conditions in the harbour entrance can present what is virtually a physical barrier to entry. More lifeboats have been lost coming back into harbour with the survivors of a rescue than in the open sea trying to effect a rescue. You have done the job, you are relaxing after the strain of rescue and then the violent waves in the entrance create the deathly finale.

Cold clear logic dictates that you should stay out at sea when there are dangerous bar conditions in the entrance but one of the problems is that you cannot always see the danger because the waves are breaking away from you towards the land. There may also be other factors. One of my most risky entrances into harbour occurred not in storm conditions but in what might have been a lazy swell rolling in from seaward off the port of St Augustine in Florida. This was not an easy entrance channel because of the dog's leg over the bar but it was marked by buoys and there seemed no real reason to worry about it. As we approached we realized that the lazy swell coming in from seaward was actually breaking very heavily on the shallow water of the bar and, to add to the difficulty, there was thick fog in the entrance, caused by the cold water coming out of the river. Suddenly we found that what looked like a nice easy entrance was very dangerous and, to add to the complexity, we were very low on fuel after running all night. Delaying entering was not an option as we would have run out of fuel waiting for conditions to improve. It was a wild ride in over the heavy breaking waves but, fortunately, we managed to pick out the channel buoys in the fog although it was a high-risk venture. The only thing in our favour was that it was not blowing a gale at the time. Add in storm conditions and we would have been in grave and possibly terminal danger.

Out on the west coast of the US there are rivers that run into the sea through shallow entrances where storms can generate fearsome conditions. These rivers are mainly in the north-west and perhaps the best known is the Columbia River where the US Coastguard have established a training base for their lifeboat crews. Here the crews learn how to take their boats through the heavy breaking surf at the river entrance, generating the most dramatic pictures of boats in wild sea conditions. It is on this bar that storm seas or the heavy swell from the aftermath breaks with a ferocity that tests lifeboat designs and their crews to the limit. Even with self-righting lifeboats the chances of survival if things go wrong in these conditions can be quite small and it is to the credit of the Coastguard that they test their boats to these limits.

Other harbours can present different dangers. Storm waves entering can be reflected from a protective stone harbour wall extending out to seaward to protect the harbour area, creating very dangerous conditions just when you think the protection of the harbour is close. Those reflected waves mix with the incoming waves to create what are called clapotic seas, where the waves take on a pyramid form, rearing up alongside with sharp breaking peaks and creating wild dangerous seas where the boat seems never able to get into step and even ships can be affected by these conditions.

For ships, conditions in harbour entrances may not present the same danger as they do to small craft but there is a different worry. Many modern designs of ships such as passenger vessels, car carriers and

> **A lifeboat of the US Coastguard during training operations on the bar of the Columbia River.**

∧ **The 44ft (13m) US Coastguard lifeboat operating in rough seas.**

container ships have very high sides that can present huge areas to a wind from the side. We have already seen how high the lateral wind pressure can be under storm conditions and trying to control these ships within the tight confines of a harbour in strong winds can be a nightmare yet they are expected to cope and keep to schedule. For the captain and the pilot it can be difficult and challenging and you only know you have made the right decision when you are safely berthed alongside without damage. These days it is the ability to manœuvre safely in harbour that can determine whether it is safe for a ferry to sail in strong winds and not necessarily what the sea conditions are like outside.

Dover harbour in Britain is one of the busiest ferry ports in the world, created by the construction of a massive stone wall. The clapotic seas off this wall are notorious for small craft as it is exposed to the south-west storm winds that prevail along this coast and the dangerous reflected seas can extend for up to a mile offshore. I have left in a Force 11 storm when testing a 44ft (13m) lifeboat and it was one of the wildest days I have spent at sea. The ferries had stopped running and it was very lonely out there on our crossing to the French port of Dunkirk. The storm seas were made worse by the strong tides that were flowing down the strait against the wind from the south-west and these were wild and unpredictable waters. At one point a big wave swept over the boat, taking the radar scanner with it, so we were reduced to visual navigation, which was made more difficult as the first buoy we found had been swept clean so there was no identification on it.

Ships may have difficulty in berthing in strong winds but these days they are expected to go to sea whatever the conditions outside and that means that services like pilot boats have to be able to cope with rough conditions in harbour entrances in order to service them. Some of the more exposed pilot stations have started to use helicopters to put pilots on board but the capability of pilot boats has improved dramatically so that they can operate in more extreme storm conditions. One pilot boat builder in Ireland believes in testing his designs to the limits in rough seas and Frank Kowalski from Safehaven Marine thinks that this is the best way to convince his customers about the capability of his designs. His account of the some sea trials follows:

"On Saturday 17th January 2009 Ireland was hit by violent storm-force 11 and hurricane wind speeds of 140kmph, 93kts were recorded. A large amount of structural damage was caused throughout the country with large areas without electricity due to fallen lines and many houses and cars were damaged by falling trees. Both roller shutter doors were blown in at our new Youghal factory, and the road to the marina was blocked by a fallen tree. As part of our efforts to record storm footage for a forthcoming TV documentary we intended to take some video footage of our pilot vessel being sea-trialled in heavy weather, but the ferocity of the storm even caught us by surprise. As we were casting off from our marina it was disintegrating around us, and even as we headed out to the harbour entrance in 'sheltered waters' the wind and sea state was amazing with 6ft waves in the inner harbour. As we made our way out to Roches Point conditions worsened and when we reached the open sea the wind was so strong that the sea appeared to smoke as if on fire as the surface of the sea was stripped off and blown along. At the start of the video Cork Harbour radio was recording 85 knots and the Grimaldi line ferry broke her moorings, going aground before being pulled off by the Harbour's tugs.

'The waves over the Harbour Rock in the entrance were phenomenal and breaking very heavily as the spring ebb tide ran out into the face of

> ### *I have left in a Force 11 storm when testing a 44ft (13m) lifeboat and it was one of the wildest days I have spent at sea.*

the Southerly seas. Wave heights recorded were 6m/20ft. We took our Interceptor 55 Pilot out through this maelstrom to demonstrate her sea keeping and capture some exceptional video footage. For sure I had to nurse her carefully trying to avoid the worst seas, although occasionally, unavoidably we would get slammed by a set of big breakers, but she looked after us and took us through it safely. Running back in with the seas behind us was 'interesting' to say the least.'

The only other boats I know that are tested to the limits like this are lifeboats but most leisure craft these days do not experience rough seas except in the hands of owners when they get caught out. Cars and aircraft get tested to virtual destruction before being handed over customers but it seems that builders do not have the courage to do this with most leisure boats.

The margins can be small in these testing conditions and any failure of the on-board systems can lead to disaster. It is the same with ships and, provided everything keeps working on board, they can normally cope. However, most operate with single engines and single steering systems. One failure in these systems and a ship can be in immediate danger.

Immobilized ships still drift ashore when engines or steering fails and a recent case was the bulk carrier *Freida* that drifted ashore at Europa Point in Gibraltar. The ship ended up right under the cliffs and, with the wind too strong for a helicopter to effect a rescue, a crane was brought in by land and, using a basket, the crew were snatched off the deck just before the ship started to break up. Off the Australian coast another bulk carrier, the *Pasha*, drifted ashore onto a beach in storm conditions when her anchor failed to hold.

Frank Kowalski testing his 55ft (17m) pilot cutter in storm conditions in Cork Harbour.

SAFEHAVEN MARINE

With the supertanker *Amoco Cadiz* it was not the main engine that failed but the steering gear. Having a working main engine on a ship of this size is not much use if you cannot point the ship in the right direction. The ship was out of control and the heroic efforts of the captain to keep it from drifting towards the shore were in vain. Thinking he could keep control of the situation in the storm conditions and that the steering gear could be repaired, he left it too late to call for help. A tug battled its way through the storm to get there before the ship went

aground and, after a struggle, a tow line was connected, parted and was connected again, all the time the ship drifting closer to land. When she finally went ashore off the coast of Brittany and started to break up it was one of the worst oil pollution disasters ever, all because the steering failed and there was no back-up.

When I first went to sea in the 1950s you would find ships anchoring in places like the Downs off the Kent coast and in Torbay and other sheltered places, waiting for storms to abate. Unless the conditions are exceptionally severe these anchorages are virtually empty these days, demonstrating how shipping is expected to keep to schedule, placing a huge responsibility on the shoulders of a captain. He gets blamed if he does not keep to time and he gets blamed if he takes a risk, does not shelter and the ship gets into difficulties in storm conditions. These shelters were used mainly by coastal shipping, deep-sea ships expected to keep going whatever the conditions. The large container ship *Napoli* was a ship that kept going down-Channel into a storm and the stress of the waves proved too much for her hull structure. When the ship started to break up the crew were taken off and the ship drifted. Eventually she was taken in tow but the structural damage was so severe that she had to be beached before she got to shelter, causing pollution and extensive damage.

Amoco Cadiz aground and breaking up off the Brittany Coast with a massive oil spill.

When I first went to sea in the 1950s you would find ships anchoring in places like the Downs off the Kent coast and in Torbay and other sheltered places.

Inshore, you cannot just let the yacht drift and wait for the storm to abate but have to battle to keep your distance from the land. Yachtsman Francis Joyon had a taste of what severe fatigue can do when, just after setting a single-handed record under sail across the Atlantic, he was returning from the English coast to his native France and he fell asleep at the helm, finally overcome by extreme tiredness. He was woken up when his big catamaran hit the rocks on the French coast at speed and he was lucky to survive.

It is in situations like this that the lifeboats provide a last line of defence for seafarers in trouble and these remarkable craft have to be prepared to put to sea when the prudent seaman stays in harbour. This demands the ultimate in seaworthiness and skill but it also has to be coupled with speed because there is so often a sense of urgency about a rescue. Speed and seaworthiness are not always happy bedfellows and with a lifeboat it is not just a case of getting to a casualty; the design has to be developed to have something extra to help those in distress. Trying to go fast in storm conditions can be a recipe for disaster and the lifeboat crews can tread a very narrow line between success and failure when on their way to a casualty. This can be a high-risk situation but the difference between a lifeboat and other small craft is that the lifeboat is designed not to fail under the severe stress of storm conditions.

Lifeboats are a good example of how man has learned to defy storms and come up with a lifesaving solution. A similar challenge faced the builders of the early lighthouses that stand sentinel to warn mariners of dangerous rocks and shoals. Even today, in a high technology world, the building of lighthouses on exposed rocks that may be barely awash and which have to stand up to the full force of the ocean storms is remarkable engineering. One of the best examples is the Bishop Rock Lighthouse located on the south-west extremity of Britain and wide open to the full force of the Atlantic Ocean. Just landing on these half-tide rocks at low water would be a challenge but the builders of this lighthouse in 1858 chipped away at the rocks to create a foundation and then laid stone after interlocking stone to create a lighthouse that has stood against the worst Atlantic storms.

Even the best harbour defences can be uprooted in extreme storms, with huge blocks of stone or concrete ripped from the seabed but

The huge wall of water created by this incoming surf is the remnant of a big storm way out at sea.

the tall, slender lighthouses stand supreme, some of the few man-made structures to do this. So exposed is the Bishop Rock Lighthouse that occasionally storm waves sweep right over it, but it remains as testimony to brilliant design and construction. Today it is serviced by helicopter but I have been to the lighthouse by boat. Just getting on board is a delicate and risky operation and gives some idea what it must have been like to build it. The bell, located 100ft (30m) above high water, was torn away in a storm. At the Unst Lighthouse to the north of Shetland a door located 195ft (59m) above the sea was broken open by storm waves.

While lighthouses would give at least some feeling of solidity, the men who manned the lightships must have suffered terribly during storms. Some lightships like the one marking the Nantucket Shoals on the US east coast and the one guarding the Seven Stones off the south-west tip of Britain were so exposed that they were moored virtually in the open ocean and had to take the full brunt of storm conditions.

When the sea meets the land, the water can release its latent energy in violent breaking waves.

When the Storms Meet the Land ■ 101

Many lightships have parted their moorings and drifted ashore or been swamped and capsized. It was a dangerous and terribly uncomfortable life and today the few remaining lightships in use are unmanned and operated by remote control.

Over the years man has tried to modify and control the effects of storms on or near land with sea defences and massive breakwaters but, at best, these man-made structures are puny when compared with the power of a storm. Robert Louis Stevenson measured the force of the sea generated by winter gales on the coast of Scotland and found that this could be as much as 6,000lbs/sq foot (29t/sq m). In 1872 the whole of the end of the breakwater at Wick in Scotland was carried away in a winter storm. The block that was moved weighed 1,350 tons and five years later its 2,600 ton replacement suffered the same fate. Now man is trying to harness some of this wave power to generate electricity but I find it hard to believe that floating structures that can withstand the mighty power of storms for long.

An example of the huge power that is contained in a wave is seen in those areas that are much sought after by the dedicated surfer. It requires a unique combination of sloping beach and deep water close in for the swell to rear up and create a huge wall of water that will roar in to the beach on Hawaii or the west coast of the US, which are prime areas for surfers. The waves come in initially as a low swell that has probably started life as the aftermath of a severe storm hundreds of miles away but when they reach the beach they can be 30 or 40ft (9–12m) high, to challenge the bravest of surfers.

When storm waves reach and are influenced by the shallows and the land they adopt a malevolent and chaotic nature that can tax the skills of the best of seamen and engineers. There is a menace about these waves inshore that is not found out in the open sea but we still tend to ignore the perils of the inshore storm, which is why we continue to have more shipping and yacht disasters close to land than out in the open seas.

> **Storm waves crashing onto a pier in the north-east of England.**

The Wild Southern Ocean

From about latitude 45ºS down to the **Antarctic** is the one ocean region in the world where the sea extends all the way round in one continuous sweep. This is the wild Southern Ocean, considered to be one of the stormiest sea areas of all. The virtually unlimited fetch of open ocean that girdles the Earth down here creates a path for a succession of depressions that follow one another from west to east, creating wild seas that are the dread of sailors. In the early days of exploration this remote region was virtually untouched except by some adventurous sailors such as Magellan who found their way south to round Cape Horn, only to head north again as rapidly as possible. It was centuries later that Australia and New Zealand were discovered and this led to a rapid increase in trade and shipping having to negotiate these dangerous seas.

Sailors have a name for these bleak and remote ocean seas. The Roaring Forties is the area between 30 and 40° S, and most ships tried to keep within this region. Even at these relatively moderate latitudes south the winds would roar and the storms would blow – but head even further south into what is known as the Fearsome Fifties and things get a lot worse. Ships would try to avoid the expanse of constant storms between 40 and 50° S but if you wanted to round Cape Horn you had no choice. Few sailors dared go further south into what is known as the Screaming Sixties – this is a bleak area where not only are there constant storms but also the hazard of ice. The names of these remote sea regions did not happen by accident and today few ships go south of the Roaring Forties. It is only those intrepid or perhaps foolish yachtsmen that head further south to find the optimum route for a quick passage across the bleak Southern Ocean.

It is a wild country down here, with only three major capes intruding southwards into these inhospitable waters. Cape Agulhas, at the southern tip of South Africa, was the first to be discovered but, at 35ºS, it is partly immune from the wild westerlies, at least in the summer months. Cape Horn, the southerly tip of South America, is at 55ºS, right in the path of the westerlies and amongst seamen it

The scale of Southern Ocean waves can be judged by the way this 700ft ship is pitching. Both crew and passengers have a tense time in these conditions.

Stormy weather at Cape Horn. Rounding the Cape is a challenge for seamen because of the gales that constantly ravage these seas.

has probably the worst reputation for stormy weather of any region on Earth. This is because it was a cape that had to be rounded to get from the Atlantic into the Pacific Ocean before the Panama Canal was built. With ships heading west it could take weeks or even months for a sailing ship to get round and ships might have to make several attempts with the fear of constantly being blown back to the Atlantic side as the next storm powered in from the west.

Almost unknown amongst these mighty southern capes is South Cape at the bottom end of New Zealand. This is as wild and remote a region as that around Cape Horn and can experience extreme weather but is well off the main shipping routes and so hardly gets a mention in the tales from the Southern Ocean. I have been down there in a yacht and to round this cape feels like heading off the edge of the world, knowing that there is only Antarctica thousands of miles to the south and virtually no shipping in between. In terms of remoteness for shipping South Cape beats them all but at least there is civilization close by to the north.

During the winter months in the Southern Ocean the storms rage. Winds of Force 7 or more can be found over the whole region for ten days or more every month. The depressions that create these winds head from west to east and the strongest winds, those from the west, will be found on the south side of a depression. The winds may be stronger here but the more difficult sea conditions can be found on the north side of a depression because they will be easterly and will create a wind against current situation that can make the waves steeper and more likely to break. To sail in this region requires a delicate balance between trying to keep in the westerly winds to make the best progress and not getting too far south where ice can be encountered coming up from the Antarctic. The further south the ships went the shorter the distance would be because the track would follow the great circle route more closely. With the benefit of today's accurate weather forecasting and good communications it should be a relatively easy job to find the optimum route to take but in the days of the clipper ships engaged on the booming trade with Australia and New Zealand it must have required all the captain's skill and knowledge to find the best route and to make the fastest passage.

It was this exposure to the dangers of Cape Horn and the Southern Ocean that was the main incentive for building the Panama Canal.

These fast clipper ships would make the journey out from Europe via Cape Agulhas and back via Cape Horn in order to use the prevailing winds to best advantage. Before the opening of the Panama Canal the trade route between the east and west coasts of North America was also around Cape Horn and it was these ships that had to battle against the prevailing violent westerlies to get round. When steam took over from sail in the mid and late 1880s, the ships were able to make passage through the Strait of Magellan just a bit to the north, an area still lashed by violent storms but less exposed to the big seas until out into the Pacific. It has been reported that the sound of the waves crashing on the weather side of the Horn peninsula can be heard 20 miles inland so that, even though they were in sheltered waters, ships making passage through the strait must have heard the ominous roar from outside.

It was this exposure to the dangers of Cape Horn and the Southern Ocean that was the main incentive for building the Panama Canal. Opening at a time when sail was in decline and steam ships were becoming the mainstay of world trade, the need to make the passage around Cape Horn and across the Southern Ocean was largely removed. The earlier opening of the Suez Canal had greatly reduced the traffic across the section of ocean between South Africa and Australia although, even in the 1950s, slower tramp ships were still using this route when cargoes were not time-critical. I have made that passage in a 6,000-ton ship and, even though we kept to the north, roughly following the 35th parallel and passing close to St Paul's Island, the storms were wild and relentless. It was a 31-day passage to Melbourne and some of the worst storms were on the last part, crossing the Great Australian Bight, where our deck cargo was washed overboard. What is scary about making a voyage across this ocean is the loneliness; you don't see another ship the whole way and, with the continuous storms, there is a feeling of the world coming to an end.

Ships still use this southern route to a limited extent but this remote ocean is now often used by yachts undergoing the ultimate test.

Ships still use this southern route to a limited extent but this remote ocean is now often used by yachts undergoing the ultimate test. Round the world yacht racing and record breaking takes the yachts mainly from Europe down to the tip of South Africa and then across the Southern Ocean to Cape Horn and back up to Europe. It is a challenging 26,000 mile journey and around half of that route is spent in the Southern Ocean. Even though most of these races and record attempts take place in the summer months of the south, the yachts can expect a wild ride in the Roaring Forties and they tread a narrow line between success and disaster. Get into trouble down here and you can be a long way from help. When racing the yachts mainly have to support each other if there are problems but when record breaking it can be very lonely out there and any help can be days away. The Australian Navy, who operate in these waters, have done some excellent rescue jobs over the years and coming to the aid of Tony Bullimore when his yacht lost its keel was a memorable event. Bullimore spent three days inside his capsized yacht before he was rescued by the navy.

To give an idea of the severity of these southern waters, in 2008 only half of the original Vendee Globe competitors were left in the race at the halfway stage. When you think that these large 60ft (18m) yachts are being sailed single-handed for 26,000 miles in the wildest waters in the world you have to wonder if this is a step too far. It is taking extreme sports to the limit and these yachts are built as light as possible for speed but still need the strength to cope with the Southern Ocean. This presents something of a nightmare

The sort of seas that can
be a daily experience in
the wild Southern Ocean.

for the designers who have to decide where the balance lies and they are always under pressure to make the boats sail faster. In single-handed sailing it is impossible to be on deck the whole time so when a larger than normal wave comes along it is too late to take action.

Jonny Malbon, who skippered *Artemis* in the race, says: 'The threat of a race-ending incident is constant. A large proportion of the time during racing in the Vendee Globe is spent on the edge. At one point I was doing 28 knots with just my staysail up. I was sitting by the hatch and the boat was completely underwater up to the mast. There was 60 knots of wind and 26ft high waves and I felt that at any time the mast could go.'

At this level, this type of racing is akin to uncontrolled madness but it is also possible to see the attraction for the competitors of having the chance to test themselves to the limits. Different skippers cope in different ways. The fact that 4,000 miles can separate the first from the last boat shows how some cope better with the pressure of the constant storms. It only takes one huge breaking storm wave to do the damage that can lead to retirement. Canadian competitor Derek Hatfield was forced to retire after being rolled by such a wave.

'It was pretty unbelievable the size of that wave. I was lying in my bunk at the time and then the next minute I was standing on the ceiling.'

Even modern ships can find the seas of the Southern Ocean a real challenge.

Hatfield reckons that the yacht was on its side for over a minute and the battering of the waves smashed the rudder system and cracked the coachroof. He was forced to head north to quieter waters in order to survey the damage and retire.

The list of yachts that suffer damage in these wild and lonely waters continues to grow. Even before anyone considered racing or record breaking there were yachtsmen such a Miles Smeeton and David Lewis who sailed their yachts down here in the spirit of adventure. Joshua Slocum had shown the way and there were many that followed in his footsteps. Almost without exception these yachts endured wild storms and suffered damage and yet still they come. Most follow the route from west to east but those looking for a tougher challenge go in the opposite direction, heading into the stormy seas. Of course it is the yachts that get damaged that tend to hit the headlines although there are many yachts out there that have crossed the Southern Ocean without problems.

Sailors such as Slocum only entered the Southern Ocean for a relatively brief period when they were rounding the Horn. Indeed, Slocum went through the Strait of Magellan rather than rounding the Horn, although it could be argued that the storms in this strait could be wilder that those at the Horn because of the strong currents and the way the wind funnels through the narrow passages. The struggle that many modern yachts have in coping with the rigours of the Southern Ocean puts the achievements of the explorer Magellan and those that followed him into perspective. Although he only briefly touched the Southern Ocean when passing through the strait and when rounding Cape Agulhas, it is worth remembering that the one vessel out of Magellan's five that completed the voyage, the *Victoria*, was only the same size as many modern yachts that make the voyage today. With two masts and limited sails it would have struggled to make any progress unless the wind was abaft the beam and there were no luxuries of any sort. The modern racing yachts that endure the Southern Ocean have a tough time but it is luxury compared with what Magellan's crews had to endure.

The Southern Ocean is one of the wildest and most remote places on Earth. This is a world of storms both in summer and winter and they come at you with no respite. The waves can regularly be the size of houses and, whilst many yachts report huge breaking waves overwhelming them, the only records of extreme waves that have been recorded in this region are those found in the Agulhas Current, which is only on the fringes of the Southern Ocean. I am convinced that there must be many more extreme waves along the storm tracks of this ocean because the conditions are perfect for their formation, but they go unrecorded because there is no one out there measuring them. Here you find nature at its rawest, a totally untamed environment where man ventures at his peril, and where storms take on a different meaning to the rest of the world's oceans.

Southern Ocean sea can provide tough conditions for even large ships.

Atlantic Ocean Storms

For seamen the **Atlantic Ocean** has an evil reputation. In the winter the storms that sweep across from west to east follow the path of the main shipping routes. In the summer the storms track further to the north but they never disappear, and ships and yachts can never be assured a smooth passage. To a certain extent this ocean turmoil has been tamed by the forecasters who can predict the weather with considerable accuracy – but knowing the weather is one thing, avoiding it is another and on this ocean there are only limited possibilities for weather routeing when you want to get across to the other side.

The Atlantic Ocean has long been the main shipping route for world trade and, ever since Columbus crossed it to discover America, ships of all shapes and sizes have used the Atlantic for developing trade. Slave ships, emigrant ships, mighty liners and numerous cargo ships have ploughed furrows across the Atlantic and many did not complete their journeys. Often those early sailing ships were small for open ocean crossings and it is hard to imagine what it must have been like on many of the crowded emigrant ships that were no more than 60 or 70 feet (18–21m) long and carrying up to 100 people. No wonder many did not survive the journey when the seas got rough.

The regular sailing ships carrying both cargo and passengers would have been larger and better equipped to cope with bad weather but, even then, the westbound voyage could have lasted for four weeks or more as ships battled the westerly gales on their voyage to North America. A more southerly route might have escaped the worst of the storms but it would have extended the journey time considerably and the captains had to find a balance between reducing the time for the voyage and finding better weather. Even in those days they would have been up against tight schedules and there were no prizes for taking a leisurely route.

The pace stepped up considerably when steam ships came on the scene. Now they could take direct routes to their destinations without much regard for the wind, although even these ships would been slowed by storms. Weather forecasts for the ocean were still non-existent and, whilst he might have clues about the weather changes

Typical of the storm conditions found in the North Atlantic.

from the visible signs, a captain would know little about the track of the depressions and the sorts of weather that they might produce. When you add in the risks from fog and icebergs it is no wonder that ships disappeared without trace in those stormy waters.

The introduction of the Plimsoll Line brought a degree of security to the ships by ensuring that they weren't overloaded and had adequate stability for normal events. The deep respect and fear of the conditions that prevailed during the winter on the north Atlantic routes can be seen from special load lines allocated to ships trading on this ocean. Winter North Atlantic (WNA) is the lowest of all the load lines and was designed to give ships that extra measure of security and stability on this stormy ocean.

Ships may have had extra stability but, if cargoes weren't secured adequately, the rolling of a ship could still put it at risk. Grain is one of the most dangerous cargoes to carry because it is as fluid as water. For grain cargoes a barrier or shifting board would be erected down the centreline of the ship to reduce the amount the cargo could move when the ship rolled. Once, when I was a young apprentice coming back to Europe from America with a cargo of grain, these shifting boards were carried away and we were left in a Force 10 storm with a 30° list and rolling close to 60°. From one minute to the next we did not know if we would capsize and it took 36 hours before the storm abated and we could relax a little.

V **Typical Atlantic sea in a storm.**

The *Flying Enterprise* was a famous casualty of the Atlantic when her cargo shifted and she listed more and more. The crew were taken off but the captain remained on board and only left the ship when she was on her beam-ends and just 30 miles from safety. It makes you wonder how many ships suffered a similar fate before radio enabled the crews in distress to call for help.

Many of the major storm systems that sweep across the Atlantic take a more northerly route, starting off in the wilds of Canada and heading round the southern tip of Greenland and on to Iceland. These are wild and relatively unfrequented waters except for the fishing fleets living a tough life up there. I spent some time off Iceland in the winter on a large ocean-going tug and it was a good day when it was blowing Force 8, just an ordinary gale. On one

It is too late for this ship to ease its speed to cope with the breaking crest. This is why there should always be a reserve of speed in storm conditions.

occasion we were standing by a large French trawler that was on fire in a Force 12 storm. They got the fire out but it makes you realize how small the margins can get when you have mechanical or other problems in these extreme conditions.

It comes as no surprise that the largest wave ever recorded by a ship was found in these waters. The 100-foot (30m) wave recorded by the Research Ship *Discovery* is recounted in the Extreme Waves chapter. The deepest depression ever recorded was found just south of Greenland in 1986. The central pressure in this record–breaking weather system was calculated at between 916 and 912mb. When you consider that the average pressure at the centre of most depressions can range between 950 and 1,000mb you can get some idea of just how deep this particular depression was. It was formed when two active depressions combined off the coast of Newfoundland and started to move east, creating a perfect storm situation. They had central pressures of 956 and 960mb which, on their own, represent very active depressions but the combined system became explosive as it moved north-east towards Greenland. A ship some distance from the centre of this monster recorded a pressure of 938mb and later another ship recorded 920mb. The winds were blowing at 65 to 70 knots and this was a very violent storm.

In 1993 a weather ship stationed to the west of Ireland recorded a pressure of 939mb in wind speeds of 70 knots and this one deepened to equal the record set in 1986. It seems likely that there are more very deep depressions lurking out there in the Atlantic but there are very few accurate recordings taken and ship readings may not be as accurate as those on land unless their barometers have been carefully calibrated. There are some ship readings on record that go lower than these 'official' record lows with ships in the Atlantic recording 925 and 921mb back in 1927 and 1870 but the accuracy may be suspect. Met Office modelling suggests that there may be even deeper lows out there with that 1993 storm down as far as 916mb. It is interesting to note that all these extreme lows have been recorded in the Atlantic, reinforcing its reputation as a violent ocean, and these extreme lows have only been exceeded by readings from the centre of tropical revolving storms, with one typhoon in 1979 producing a low of 870mb.

As a general rule, the deeper the depression, the stronger the winds. At around 55° N there are some areas of the Atlantic where there can be an average of 20 to 30 per cent of the time when the wind is blowing a gale in the winter months. It is in this same region that there can be waves of 13ft (4m) or more for up to 60 per cent of the time. It is not hard to understand why the Atlantic has such a reputation for bad weather and it is difficult to imagine how the early explorers and seamen coped with these extreme conditions. Fishermen from Europe have been sailing across the Atlantic to the prolific fishing waters off Newfoundland, Greenland and Iceland for hundreds of years and they must have endured appalling conditions. The death toll amongst the Grand Banks fishermen was very high and they had to contend with violent storms as well as the extreme cold. When I was north of Iceland in the 1980s I also encountered the double jeopardy of storms and the ship icing up in the freezing temperatures.

One area of the North Atlantic that has a particularly evil reputation amongst seamen is the Bay of Biscay. The reputation stems from the days when sailing ships were in danger of becoming embayed in a westerly storm. This is a deep bay along the French and Spanish coasts with Ushant pointing out into the Atlantic to the north and Cape Finisterre to the south. Running between these two headlands in a westerly gale there was always a real risk of ships being set into the bay and having no way out. These days, with powered ships, there is always a way out but the wild seas remain and so does the Bay of Biscay's evil reputation. At the edge of the bay the Continental Shelf starts to rise up from the ocean depths and this causes the deep ocean swells to shorten their wavelength and turn into nasty surface waves. For modern ships the Bay is a challenge but for yachts and small craft the reputation is such that insurance companies are still reluctant to give insurance cover for traversing the bay in the winter months. Even in the summer there is always a sigh of relief after the bay has been crossed and the more predictable coastal conditions take over.

Ships tend to take the most direct Great Circle route that follows a curve to the north across the Atlantic, so they are very much in the firing line of the storms. Weather routeing will help them to miss the extremes and, indeed, this routeing aims to find a compromise between the shortest route and the one where the ship can maintain the fastest speed. Yachts that are not in a hurry tend to follow a more southerly route across the Atlantic where they engage with the Azores High and should get good sailing winds. This more southerly route may be longer but it also avoids the powerful Gulf Stream when heading west, which can slow progress considerably when sailing. Cruising yachts can afford this leisurely progress but when racing or record breaking, sailboats tend to work much closer to the weather limits. Record breaking under power needs calm seas but under sail you try to balance on the knife edge between fast progress and wild seas. You want the strong winds for speed but you don't want the big seas that go with them as the waves slow progress. It is a delicate balance between the two and record breaking yachts aim to hitch a ride on the back or front of a fast-moving depression where the wind is on the beam from the north or south. Trying to keep in the right position for the six or seven days required for a record requires good forecasting and on the one attempt I made at a record, when we were riding the front of a deep depression, we got out of step and hit the violent 70 knot winds of the intense part of the depression and ended up having to be rescued.

I have crossed the Atlantic in many types of boat and ship and I don't recall an easy or relaxed passage. Even when you skirt the edges, if you are heading along the shores of North America or crossing the Bay of Biscay, you can meet severe weather conditions. For centuries the Atlantic has been the main trade route of the world and it has taken its toll on ships and shipping. Those who take the Atlantic and its wild weather lightly are likely to find themselves in serious trouble and the ocean floor must be littered with shipping that did not make it.

A line squall like this can turn placid seas into violent waves within a very short time.

Indian Ocean Monsoons

Pictures of the Indian Ocean suggest islands with palm trees and placid waters. It can be like that but the reality, as for all oceans, is that there can be wild and raging seas as well as idyllic calms. The Indian Ocean is unique in that it plays host to the monsoon, a weather feature that brings life to the Indian subcontinent but storms to the surrounding sea areas. The unique feature of the monsoon is that it is not only seasonal and completely reverses with the change of season but it appears with a regularity and consistency that can be relied on. In terms of weather this is almost unknown but this also means there is no escaping the monsoon storms.

It is the south-west monsoon that brings the strong winds and rough seas. These winds are generated by a consistent low pressure over the Indian subcontinent that combines with high pressure over the trade wind zone to the south. The air flows from the high pressure to the low pressure regions and the steady winds of the monsoon are fed by the SE trade winds and then accelerate towards the Indian subcontinent. The high and low pressure zones create what is a permanent downhill slope for the air and the wind strength can vary between Force 6 and Force 8; not quite storm strength but the sheer consistency of these winds makes this region a storm zone that can make life at sea very uncomfortable.

These monsoon winds appear on almost the same day at any one place every year, moving up from the south, and because they have travelled over warm moist seas they bring heavy rain and relief from the dry heat. It is the rain for which the monsoon is best known but for seamen the strong and steady winds can knock up a very nasty sea. The waves are larger than would normally be expected from such a constant wind from the same direction. The trading dhows that entered the Arabian Sea region from the Arabian Gulf would avoid the region during the monsoon season and, indeed, the word monsoon originates from the Arabic. The south-west

Monsoon conditions in the Arabian Sea.

The winds that cause the monsoon storms in the Indian Ocean.

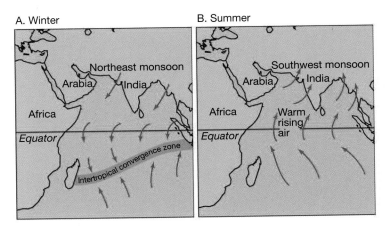

A. Winter — Northeast monsoon — Arabia — India — Africa — Equator — Intertropical convergence zone

B. Summer — Southwest monsoon — Arabia — India — Africa — Warm rising air — Equator

monsoon season begins in June and lasts through to October. For the rest of the year the wind is reversed, blowing off the land and out to sea. However, whilst these north-east monsoon winds may be as strong, the sea conditions are considerably reduced because the wind is blowing off the land. Similar monsoon conditions can be found in south-east Asia bordering northern Australia and in equatorial Africa but the sea conditions generated by these winds do not match those found in the Arabian Sea.

A dangerous side effect of the monsoon winds occurs at the beginning and end of the south-west monsoon season – the development of tropical cyclones. These may not have the frequency of the Atlantic or Pacific hurricanes but they can be equally damaging. They tend to be found mainly towards the end of the monsoon season in October and November, forming just to the north of the equator and heading up either side of the Indian peninsula. Those moving to the west of the peninsula into the Arabian Sea tend to be dying out by the time they reach land but those that head up into the Bay of Bengal can be particularly damaging because the bay is surrounded by land. For shipping this means possible escape routes can be blocked by land so that the room for negotiation with storms is limited. These cyclones can occur throughout the south-west monsoon season from April to November but their number tends to be limited to four or five a year.

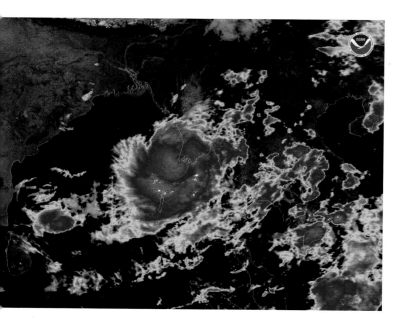

A violent cyclone moving up into the Bay of Bengal.

As far as storms are concerned the main area of excitement in the Indian Ocean is to the north of the equator. South of the equator, the weather can also be enlivened by cyclones. Here the cyclone season starts in December, running through to April, and they are spread right across the Indian Ocean from Australia to the African coast. They have decidedly southerly courses and most head down to join the procession of Southern Ocean storms and turn into extra-tropical depressions. From a news point of view these storms have only a small impact because there is little in the way of land for them to hit except for the islands of Mauritius, Reunion and Madagascar. For shipping, however, crossing this ocean

before radio communications and good forecasting was rather like a game of Russian Roulette.

The effect of the powerful Agulhas Current meeting the strong westerly or south-westerly winds that come into the Indian Ocean from the southern seas has already been mentioned. This is the typical wind against current situation that can transform normal gale-generated seas into a dangerous maelstrom of breaking waves and deep holes that have been the death of many ships. Just outside the Indian Ocean region, the sea conditions at the extremity of South Africa are made worse by the Agulhas Bank, an area of shallow water that extends south from Cape Agulhas. There is little record of the loss of shipping that must have occurred in this region in the early days of exploration but the sea conditions during strong winds must have been very challenging for the small sailing ships of the time.

The Indian Ocean is an ocean of contrasts. In most of the other ocean areas you expect rough seas and storms but the Indian Ocean generally offers good sailing. Storms come as an unpleasant surprise, which can make them all the more dangerous, and it is only at the southern end when you head into the Roaring Forties that things liven up with regular and damaging storm conditions.

Typical monsoon storm conditions in the indian Ocean.

Pacific Ocean Cyclones

The Pacific Ocean is anything but peaceful, despite the name. The largest ocean on the planet has its relatively quiet and predictable areas in the trade wind belt but it is also host to some of the wildest weather on Earth. Like the Atlantic, the moderate conditions are found on each side of the equator but head up into higher latitudes and you find stormy seas that rival anything anywhere else. To the south the Pacific merges into the Southern Ocean where the storms rage relentlessly from west to east. In the north there is a similar pattern but the much shorter fetch creates a different type of dangerous sea, making the waters around the Aleutian Islands and the Bering Sea some of the most feared areas in the world.

Most of the storms in the north are generated by the procession of low-pressure systems that start north of Japan and head out across the Pacific. The conditions to the north of the Aleutian Islands have been vividly portrayed in the TV series *The Deadliest Catch* and for the crews of the fishing fleets that operate in these seas the risks are considered to be among the highest of any occupation. US Coastguard statistics show that over 50 per cent of the fishing boat casualties are caused by storms or capsizes in rough seas and in these northern waters the survival times in the water can be minutes, with help a long way off. Since survival suits have become compulsory the chances of survival have risen but there is an ever-present danger because the storms often bring blizzards and the icing-up of a ship's structure can have a major effect on its stability. Rather like the northern waters of the Atlantic, the main fishing areas appear to be in the stormiest waters and you have to wonder if the fish do not have an instinct for survival by being most plentiful in the most dangerous seas.

In 1982 a Japanese trawler capsized in Alaskan waters, drowning all 32 of her crew, and this was followed in 2001 by the 92ft (28m) long *Arctic*

13

The two halves of the *Selendang Ayu* ashore off the coast of Alaska.

A fishing boat operating in storm conditions in the Bering Sea.

Rose, which sank in rough seas with the loss of all 15 of her crew. It is claimed that the *Arctic Rose* had both mechanical and stability problems that were exacerbated by the storm conditions. In 1985 a 70 year old fishing vessel sank after leaving Kodiak in Alaska with the loss of six lives – you wonder what a boat of this vintage was doing operating in these wild waters. Fishing vessel safety is reckoned to be poorly regulated in the US and this is claimed to be partly responsible for the high incidence of casualties in these northern waters, only wanting one relatively minor failure in storm conditions to start a vessel on the long downhill slope to disaster.

The cargo ship *Helena II* went aground in a storm off the coast of Japan in 2005 and three injured crewmen were taken off a chemical tanker that had an encounter with an extreme wave 200 miles south of the Aleutian Islands in 2008. The *Cougar Ace* was a car carrier that was reported to have been struck by a large wave during a ballast transfer operation whilst on passage south of the Aleutians in 2006, causing her to develop a 60° list. The crew were rescued and the ship was towed to harbour and salvaged. One of the most epic storm stories of this region in modern times was the battle to save the *Selendang Ayu*, which struggled through storm-force winds on its way from Seattle to China. The optimum route for this voyage takes ships north of the Aleutians, and the *Selendang Ayu* was battling big seas when the engine failed and the ship eventually went aground. All the crew were rescued but the ship broke up and sank.

Even large fishing boats can be vulnerable in storms in the Bering Sea.

Unlike the relatively open waters of the Atlantic, the northern Pacific region is littered with islands and it seems likely that these have an effect on the nature of the waves that are generated by the storms. Anything that interferes with the smooth flow of waves and water will affect their size and shape and while there have been only a few reports of extreme waves in this region, this could be because of the lack of means of measuring them rather than their non-existence. All of the ingredients for larger than normal waves exist in this region but there are no weather or research ships or buoys out there to make measurements

and, apart from inshore Alaska waters, this is an area where cruise ships have yet to venture.

> **The Bering Sea has been the graveyard of many ships.**

I am sure that there are research ships operating in the Pacific but it has over 25,000 islands, more than all the other oceans put together. These are all potential weather reporting stations so the weather patterns of the Pacific are well understood but the heights of waves cannot be measured from islands so these statistics go unrecorded.

Again belying its peaceful name, the Pacific has a higher number of tropical storms than any other ocean. This is the only ocean where these storms occur on both the eastern and western sides so, throughout the year, there is a risk of these violent storms occurring somewhere in this vastness. South of the equator they form amongst the proliferation of islands around the International Date Line and then head mainly south or south-west. Only those to the west, near Australia and New Zealand, cause much concern to shipping but this is a popular region for cruise shipping and there have been several encounters between cruise ships and the big waves generated by these storms.

Again belying its peaceful name, the Pacific has a higher number of tropical storms than any other ocean.

The *Pacific Star* sailed into a cyclone between Australia and Vanuatu and, in the heavy seas, a number of passengers were injured and damage was done to internal fittings. The passengers suggested that the incident was caused by the captain trying to keep to a schedule in the storm conditions. A year before, the same ship ran into a similar storm with 50 knot winds after leaving Auckland in New Zealand and in 2008 a sister ship had a similar experience. All this shows how this region is susceptible to strong winds and rough seas and the north-east coast of Australia is battered annually by one or more cyclones. Indonesia, to the north, with its many islands, is also very much in the firing line of the cyclones and there have been many casualties after ferries have been caught out in the fierce storms.

The Philippines, further north, lie in the path of many of the tropical storms that form north of the equator and which later curve around to threaten China and Japan. Like Indonesia, there have been many cases of inter-island ships in the Philippines sailing into storms and capsizing or grounding with high loss of life. The sheer density of shipping increases the risk of casualties but you cannot help feeling that there is a reluctance to cancel scheduled voyages even though a storm is imminent.

By the time these tropical storms reach the crowded seas off the Chinese and Japanese coasts they tend to be well-recorded and their track well-predicted so there should be adequate warning and time for ships and small vessels to seek shelter or to take avoiding action.

The tropical storms on the east side of the Pacific tend to head up the coast from Central America but some disappear out into the wide blue yonder of the Pacific's open spaces before they die out. These occur during the same period as the Caribbean hurricanes and some think that they may be a continuity of the same storms after they have passed over the narrow land belt of Central America.

The impact of the Southern Ocean storms is felt down south and, as in northern waters, some of the intense low-pressure areas will curve towards the equator rather than following their regular eastward path. Some of the storms that seem to regularly affect the yachts participating in the famous Sydney to Hobart Race are created by secondary low-pressure areas that form at relatively short notice and can have vicious twists in their tails with winds of 50 knots or more. The 1998 race, when

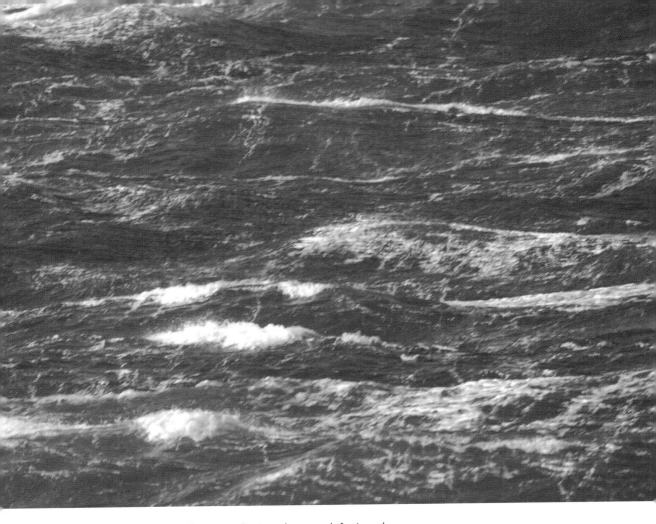

six yachtsmen died and many yachts were lost or damaged, featured winds of 80 knots and waves up to 60ft (18m) in height.

Like every ocean on the globe, the Pacific has its wild and unpredictable side. Although the weather patterns have now been tamed to a certain extent by good and generally accurate forecasting, the sheer scale of the ocean and the remoteness of many areas still make this a challenging ocean for ships and boats. Apart from the heroes who take on the Southern Ocean sector, most yachts stick to moderate latitudes. There is regular yachting traffic between the US west coast and Hawaii and that is an exposed section of ocean with nowhere to hide if the weather takes a turn for the worse. Up in the north it is really wild country and it is there that traffic is increasing with the growth in trade between the US and Asia. How long will it be before the cruise liners start to look at the Bering Sea as the new adventure cruise area with the consequent risks involved in these stormy waters?

∧ **Strong local winds can generate a very short, steep sea of considerable violence.**

Regional and Local Winds

The general pattern of winds and storms around the world is further complicated by some much more local weather effects that can be a danger to shipping and, more particularly, to small craft where any change in conditions can have a sudden dramatic effect. These local winds come in many shapes and sizes and they range from temporary gusts of increased wind strength right through to winds that affect areas hundreds of miles wide. These regional winds are almost invariably caused by local differences in temperature that give rise to changing conditions, or by the meeting of winds from different directions. This can result in some very intense, violent winds. Although the short-term nature of some of these systems often means that there will not be a significant change in the associated sea conditions, one of the dangers of these local winds is that they can be difficult to forecast accurately and they can produce dangerous conditions at short notice.

Squalls are among the best known local winds and are generated by a variety of conditions. Thunderstorms can also be very local and very intense and their mass of turbulent air generates squalls which, at the surface, can produce wind speeds of 50 or 60 knots. Whilst the possibility of thunderstorms can be forecast in general terms, the specific location of thunderstorms can only be observed visually. The main danger signal of an approaching thunderstorm is a large, rapidly growing cumulus cloud with a large characteristic anvil-shaped cloud growing out of the top. This anvil cloud tends to point in the direction in which the upper wind is blowing and this indicates the direction it is moving. At night the lightning is the best thunderstorm signal.

There are two types of thunderstorm: the heat storm and the frontal storm. Heat-generated thunderstorms are triggered by the rising air that comes from intense heating of the land. This is the type of storm you find in summer months – when the rising air draws in warm moist air at the bottom you have the ingredients for a thunderstorm. They usually form in light wind conditions, which makes them all the more dangerous because of the rapid changes in wind speed when the storm comes, and they tend to form over land initially and then drift out to sea.

A violent waterspout approaching – this is the marine equivalent of a tornado, with violent winds close to the funnel.

A frontal thunderstorm is a different animal altogether and tends to be associated with very active cold fronts. Here you can get rapidly-rising air currents because the cold air from the cold sector of the front is pushing forwards and under the warm air, causing it to rise. In a very active front this warm air can rise quickly and the situation becomes intensified if there is a considerable difference between the temperature of the air in the cold and warm sectors. The front will also be more active if the angle between the winds in the tail end of the warm sector and the front end of the cold sector is considerable, perhaps approaching 90°. Cold front thunderstorms can occur as a series of storms, sometimes closely linked together along the line of the front. This means that if the front is passing across your location you may only experience one thunderstorm but if its length is passing your position you could be in for a series of thunderstorms one after the other which would appear to merge into one long thunderstorm. Unlike the heat thunderstorms, frontal thunderstorms tend to be more frequent in the winter months simply because there are more depressions, hence more cold fronts, and they tend to be more frequent out at sea than on the land.

In general, thunderstorms occur most frequently in the summer and, although they can occur by both day and night, they tend to be more frequent in the late afternoon or early evening, particularly over inland or coastal waters. This is when the land has had the maximum time to heat up and initiate the strong convection currents. Over the ocean, thunderstorms tend to be more frequent between midnight and sunrise and the most frequent and violent thunderstorms will be found in sub-tropical latitudes.

Ahead of a thunderstorm the wind will be steady if it is a frontal thunderstorm, and it is more likely to be light and variable if it is a heat storm. As the roll cloud at the lower edge of the advancing storm comes closer the wind will tend to weaken and become variable but as it passes overhead you can expect to find violent winds coming from various directions, often accompanied by strong downdraughts. This is an area of considerable turbulence and the wind can reach speeds of 60 knots or more. Just behind this violent wind you can expect to find heavy rain, or sometimes hail.

A feature identified in some of the more severe thunderstorms is a microburst. Although most of the air is being drawn up into the thunder cloud, the violent turbulence inside the cloud leads to dense columns of cold sinking air which come down from the cloud and spread out in

all directions when they hit the surface. Winds of up to 120 knots have been measured in some of these microbursts, which may only last for a few minutes but can be devastatingly strong as far as sailing yachts are concerned, leading to a knock down or a dismasting.

Lightning, a feature of thunderstorms, can be quite frightening when it is in close proximity, and the peals of thunder that follow it add to the general feeling of threat and tension. If you can count the seconds between the flash of lightning and the noise of the thunder and divide this number of seconds by five it will give you an approximate distance off in statute miles. You should be close enough to see the storm anyway, although this could be a useful guide at night time. Radar can also give you early warning of a thunderstorm approaching as the storm itself will make a very strong target on the radar. You should be

There can be violent winds inside thunderstorms.

able to pick up the storm 20 miles or more away and you will be able to plot its progress quite accurately.

Line squalls can also produce violent winds and, like some thunderstorms, are generally associated with the passage of cold fronts rather than warm ones. Indeed, a line squall could be considered as a very direct and positive manifestation of the line of a cold front, producing visual evidence of the change from warm to cold air and physical evidence of the turbulence and violent interface between this warm and cold air.

You can't mistake a line squall with its line of dark grey, almost black cloud extending from horizon to horizon. It is usually very clearly defined and often has the appearance of a black arch across the sky with a watery, hazy look across it. Such cloud can look threatening and is the main warning sign that you can expect very turbulent wind conditions. Once you are close or under the line squall, the wind speed can rise very rapidly, often with squall-like suddenness, and at the same time there can be a considerable change in wind direction. Just to add to the misery there is usually heavy rain, sometimes hail and quite often thunder and lightning. The heavy rain can reduce visibility quite severely, perhaps to a quarter of a mile or less, resulting in a combination of poor visibility and strong, sometimes violent, winds. These can be very trying conditions but they normally last for no longer than half an hour before some sort of normality returns.

The violent conditions that generate both thunderstorms and line squalls can also be the breeding ground for a much rarer phenomenon: the waterspout. This is the ocean equivalent of the tornado but is generally less violent. They are found much more frequently in warm tropical waters but don't rule them out completely from temperate climates.

A characteristic of the sort of cloud which can produce waterspouts is the very black thunderstorm or line squall type of cloud without visible rain descending from it. Instead there may be what are known as 'mamma' which look rather like cow's teats hanging down below the cloud at intervals and visibly moving or swaying. These mamma appear to be the embryo waterspouts and, as you watch, one or more of them will change into the characteristic funnel-shaped cloud that gradually extends down towards the sea beneath. Some waterspouts may not reach the sea surface but appear to remain suspended from the clouds whilst those that do extend down to the sea will throw up spray and cause a very local area of agitated sea around the base. Waterspouts don't usually descend vertically but will often adopt quite a curve, particularly at the top end where it joins the cloud. Once fully formed, the waterspout will advance with the cloud and it may last anything from five minutes to half an hour before it becomes unstable, when it will appear to break well above the sea surface and rapidly disperse.

Waterspouts normally descend from clouds that are about 1,000ft (300m) above the sea surface and they are usually very slim. The diameter of the waterspout can be as little as 20ft (6m) or as large as 200ft (60m) in diameter where it touches the water. There is considerable reduced air pressure in the centre of this base area, which causes the sea to rise around the contact point, although this rise will be largely hidden by the amount of spray which is flying around. For yachts, both power and sail, waterspouts are something to be avoided because winds within the spout can be up to 100mph. The waterspout probably travels at around about 20mph so it shouldn't be too difficult to take avoiding action, although the movement of the waterspout where it contacts the water can be rather erratic. The best solution is to give the waterspout as wide a berth as possible, even turning around and running away from it although this can be difficult if you are in a narrow channel. If it looks as though you are going to have a close encounter with a waterspout make sure you get all the sails down and stowed, get all openings closed off and make sure all the crew are inside the boat under cover. I have been on a ship that encountered multiple waterspouts and there was no avoiding all of them. As one passed over the ship it damaged awnings and light structures but there were no major breakages. Small craft would not get away so lightly.

Thunderstorms, line squalls and waterspouts are all recognized weather phenomena associated with certain weather conditions but there are other strong wind conditions that can arrive without much notice. Gusts are found in almost all wind conditions and are temporary increases in wind speed. You like to think of winds blowing

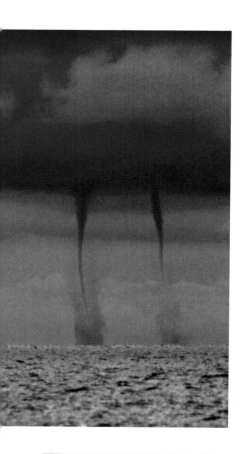

Twin waterspouts dropping from a line squall.

at a nice steady speed and the weather forecasts reinforce this view. However, this picture of steady winds is a long way from reality as the local wind speed can vary over quite a range. In strong winds of, say, Force 7 you can find the wind speed increasing by half as much again in short bursts. This is much more likely to happen near land where the topography can interfere with the airflow and, whilst the short term nature of these gusts can affect sailboats, there will be little change in the sea conditions because of the very short-term nature of the gusts.

More dangerous are the squalls that seem to appear out of nowhere. Apart from the defined squalls mentioned earlier, squalls of considerable intensity can often be found in the lee of high ground. Not only does the uneven nature of the land interfere with the smooth flow of the air but it can also generate eddies. Some of these can be extremely violent and because you are in the lee of the land where you expect to find shelter they can catch you by surprise. I was sailing in the lee of the island of Arran in the Clyde estuary when we were struck by a violent squall that turned us through 360° and laid us over on our beam ends. It was over almost before it began but it was a frightening experience. Another time when it was a raging gale outside we found what we thought was a snug anchorage in a sheltered bay with high mountains protecting us to windward. Suddenly a wall of white water headed across the bay, it hit us like a sledgehammer and there were more to follow. This eddy squall had accelerated down off the mountain and it was time to move out from what we thought was a nice sheltered anchorage.

To add to the complication of these local weather phenomena there are dangerous wind conditions that are only found in certain regions of the world. In the Mediterranean the one to avoid is the Mistral, the well-known wind that sweeps down the Rhône valley and makes life miserable in the Gulf of Lion and out into a wider area of the Mediterranean. The Mistral is what is known as a katabatic wind, a cold wind that descends a valley under the force of gravity to take the place of warmer air that is rising over the sea. It is something like a land breeze but in the case of the Mistral the speed of the wind is increased by high pressure to the north and low pressure to the south over the Mediterranean, allowing it to increase with quite dramatic force. It can reach over 80 knots in the gulf and its influence can spread over much of the western Mediterranean. The Mistral caught up with me on a delivery trip on the world's first deep-V hull, a fast patrol boat for the Greek Navy. It was a good test for this new design and I was grateful that we had the speed to run away from the storm and find shelter in Palma. There is a similar wind that can be found in the northern part of the Adriatic Sea, the Bora, the cold wind flowing down from the Alps.

Being surrounded by land, the Mediterranean has many local winds but only a few strong ones. The Scirocco is a southerly wind found in the central Mediterranean Sea that can reach gale force and the Gregale is a north-easterly that can last for several days with winds up to gale force around Malta. Like the Mediterranean, the Arabian Gulf is virtually landlocked and has its own share of local winds but these rarely reach gale force.

Towards the end of a monsoon there is a wind called the Elephanta that blows from the south or the south-east along the Malabar coast of India and in the Malacca Strait the Sumatra wind brings violent squalls and heavy rain. Off the Congo and Guinea coasts of west Africa there are violent storms that are called tornadoes but which bear no relation to the tornadoes found over the land in the US and in Australia. These African tornadoes are more like thunder squalls that travel from east to west – they start very suddenly and may only last for 15 minutes but can cause considerable damage both on land and at sea.

In South America 'williwaws' is the name given to the very violent squalls that can be found in the Strait of Magellan. These are experienced mainly in the winter months when the gales from the west tend to move north and the wind is funnelled through the narrow channels with the high land adding impetus to the violence of the squalls.

Australia has its own brands of violent winds: the Brickfielder and the Southerly Buster. These two have the same origins and are formed when a depression has changed from its normal roundish shape into one that is more pear-shaped. This creates a V at the equator end of the low pressure area, leading to very strong local winds that will change direction very suddenly as the frontal systems pass through. The Brickfielder is the wind coming off the land and tends to bring heat and dust in its train while the Southerly Buster is the wind that comes in from the south after the fronts have passed through. It is believed that it was an intense storm of this nature that caused the havoc among the competing yachts in the 1998 Sydney to Hobart Race.

In South America 'williwaws' is the name given to the very violent squalls that can be found in the Strait of Magellan.

A fully formed waterspout – there will be very violent winds around its base.

Wild Water and Whirlpools

Some parts of the world's seas are so dangerous that seamen try to avoid them at all costs. Storms on their own are bad enough but when you add in strong currents and tides the water can begin to boil, producing conditions where small craft fight to survive and even ships get into trouble. We have seen how the waves can become steeper and dangerous to shipping in the powerful Agulhas Current off South Africa but that current is only running at a couple of knots. Imagine how much worse things might get if the current is running at 10 knots or more into the teeth of a westerly gale. The waves become impossibly steep and breaking and the whole sea becomes wall to wall white water that can quickly overwhelm small craft. Conditions like this exist in many parts of the world and where the current is exceptionally strong you can get whirlpools added to the mixture.

Some of the worst sea conditions are to be found in Scottish waters. This is partly due to the geography of the region, the seas at the north of Scotland providing pathways for water filling and emptying the North Sea at every tide. Combine this with the fact that these waters are open to the wrath of the north Atlantic storms and you have a recipe for wild water. Lying across the path of the incoming and outgoing water flow are a series of islands, and the huge volumes of water have to find passages between these islands so the tides run strongly. The Pentland Firth is the narrow channel that lies between the Scottish mainland and Orkney and it feeds the North Sea with some of the strongest tidal flows in the world, running at a steady 12 knots on spring tides and stronger still in some of the eddies.

The main channel is some five miles wide but because there are islands in the middle of the channel the water flow is further complicated. The island of Stroma lies right across the water flow and further east are the Pentland Skerries. These interrupt the flow and create wild eddies that can be a danger to shipping with the transition between the main flow and the eddy so sudden in some places that it can spin a ship round. Even when there is no wind blowing, the firth is a dangerous place but add the complication of a westerly gale and things get worse. Out to the west there is a tide

A satellite image of the Strait of Messina between Sicily and Italy, showing the dangerous waves that can develop.

A tidal race is giving this
ship a rough ride.

race, the Merry Men of Mey, and this extends right across the firth from St John's Point in the south to Tor Ness on Orkney. If you are making passage through the firth there is no escaping this tide race, no quiet passage close inshore, and in a westerly gale with the ebb tide running to the west through the firth it boils. The waves are violent, they can rise very suddenly and from all directions so it is impossible to anticipate them. The pilot guide for the area is very categoric: 'Small craft should not attempt passage through the Pentland Firth except at slack water'. And this is without taking into account the effects of strong winds.

Pilot guides are not noted for emotive language so when one says 'In the terrific gales that usually occur 4 or 5 times a year, all distinction between air and water in lost', you know that they are talking about exceptional conditions. In the days when I was testing lifeboats the Pentland Firth looked like the perfect proving ground; after all, a lifeboat might have to go into that tide race to rescue another boat in trouble. The boat was a new design of 70-footer (21m) and we motored down from Shetland overnight into the teeth of a westerly gale and entered the firth early the next morning. To get a better view of what lay ahead I was in the open upper conning position as we approached the Merry

Men of Mey from the west. You could see the white water of the breaking waves ahead and, with the wind behind us, things did not look too bad. Then we were in amongst the white water and it was like being inside a washing machine. We were tossed in every direction and that big heavy 70-footer felt like a cockleshell. I put on full power to get out of this mess as quickly as possible and suddenly the boat was virtually overwhelmed. That compact, upper steering position was surrounded by water and the rest of the boat had submerged! I really thought we were going down but the boat rose out of the wave, seemed to shake itself and we were back on track. The Merry Men extended for about five or six standing waves of severe turmoil and then, like magic, it was calm on the other side. Those breaking waves take the force out of the incoming waves but, even so, we were glad and relieved to get into the fully sheltered waters of Scapa Flow.

If you survive that part of the Pentland Firth there is more to follow as you head east. The tide can run so strongly around the islands that, seen from the air, it looks as though they have a bow wave, and this creates enormous eddies running to leeward. On the flood tide these can extend a couple of miles out into the North Sea so the breaking seas will try to get you one way or the other. At slack water it can be a different story. I have been through the firth in a racing boat when we were doing the Round Scotland Powerboat Race and it was virtually

> ## *The tide can run so strongly around the islands that, seen from the air, it looks as though they have a bow wave.*

A tidal bore racing up a river in a wall of breaking water.

The Bore" Alaska Railroad Scene

Portland Race in storm conditions. Shallow water makes this tidal race especially dangerous.

a flat calm all the way but that is very rare. Ships use this channel regularly and a chemical tanker that broke down in the firth was lucky that it was in moderate conditions and there was time to take it in tow before disaster occurred.

Further to the north there is the Sumburgh Race that extends out from the southern tip of Shetland. This is just a regular tide race but in a westerly gale the seas boil and it is no place for a small boat. It is where the loaded tanker *Braer* came ashore when it lost power as it was transiting the passage from the North Sea into the Atlantic and it caused enormous pollution problems.

The Portland Race off the south coast of Britain is a similar type of tide race but made more dangerous because of the shallow water. Once again, this race, which extends some four miles out from the headland, is a dangerous place for small craft. For those who know the way there is a narrow passage inshore where the waves do not break but to negotiate this you need to be very close in. Just a quarter of a mile off the point you can see the breaking seas that threaten to engulf a small craft. Like so many of these tide races, the area of breaking water changes with the tide and off Portland you can find that, just when you think you have made a safe passage through the race, you meet up with a powerful eddy that curls around to meet the main stream again and creates a dangerous patch of breaking waves in the lee of the headland.

Tide races can form around many headlands where the tidal stream runs strongly but they can also be found in many narrow channels where the tidal flow is squeezed between the sides of the channel as it narrows. The really vicious tide races tend to occur in narrow inlets that are backed up by extensive areas of water. What is claimed to be the fastest flow in the world occurs in the Skookumchuck Narrows in British Columbia. The entrance is some 330yds (300m) wide but it is the only channel for three inlets from the sea: the main Sechelt Inlet and the offshoots called the Narrows and Salmon Inlets. This means that a considerable body of water has to flow through the narrows on each tide with the current running at up to 20 knots. The water boils even in calm weather and the rapids are a big tourist attraction.

Coming a close second is the Saltstraumen in the north of Norway. Here it is calculated that every six hours over 400 million tonnes of water have to pass each way through a channel that is 1.5 miles long and just 150m wide. It is claimed that the current runs at up to 22 knots, making it faster than the Skookumchuck, and both of these rapids lay claim to being the world's fastest. The Saltstraumen also has significant whirlpools in the rapids and these are most apparent near the side of the channel where the water is slowed by the banks and

Crowds watch the Skookumchuck tide race in British Columbia.

An old map showing the Moskenstraumen as a coiled up sea serpent.

the faster current drags the water into whirlpools. These whirlpools or vortices are actually quite small, perhaps up to 30ft (10m) in diameter, but on a strong tide day they can look quite daunting.

A much larger whirlpool, the Old Sow, is also found in Canada, this time on the east coast off Deer Island in New Brunswick. This area is on the edge of the Bay of Fundy, which has the biggest tidal range in the world at over 15m (50ft) so the flow of water in and out of the enclosed bay is considerable. Combine this with the uneven bottom features and the tide flow creates a whirlpool that is estimated at being over 250ft (75m) in diameter. In addition to the whirlpool there are standing waves in the area and several smaller whirlpools. Nearby in the Bay of Fundy there are reversing falls on the St John's River, created by the extreme rise and fall of the tide.

The most famous of all whirlpools is the Moskenstraumen that forms in the waters near the end of the Lofoten islands off the coast of northern Norway. Compared with the location of the other whirlpools, this one is an open ocean location in a relatively wide channel over 2 miles wide.

The whirlpool is named after the island in the middle of the channel, Mosken, and the flow in the channel has been measured at over 15 knots. The *Norwegian Pilot Guide* is graphic in its description. 'Though rumour has greatly exaggerated the importance of the Maelstrom or more properly the Moskenstraumen that runs between Mosken and Lofotodden it is still the most dangerous tideway in Lofoten, its violence being due in great measure to the irregularity of the ground. As the strength of the tide increases the sea becomes heavier and the current more irregular, forming extensive eddies or whirlpools. During such periods no vessel should enter the Moskenstraumen.'

This is the whirlpool that has featured in works of fiction such as Edgar Allen Poe's *A Descent into the Maelstrom* and Jules Verne's *Twenty Thousand Leagues Under the Sea*. The Lofoten islands stretch out from the coastline of Norway like a giant hook and they form an obstruction to the tidal currents that flow up and down this coastline. It is this flow through the channels between the islands at the tip of the Lofotens that creates the tide race. It is not just the currents that create the upheaval in this region because it is also wide open to the storms that sweep in from the Atlantic so the whole area is one of wild water. The Lofoten islands are not far from the area where the Norwegian weather ship *Polar Front* met up with the 90ft (27m) wave mentioned in the Extreme Waves chapter.

Another famous whirlpool is found off the west coast of Scotland. The Gulf of Corryvreckan is a narrow channel that runs between the Sound of Jura and the open ocean and the whirlpool here is reckoned to be the third largest in the world. The underwater features combine with the strong tidal flow to create the whirlpool: a pillar of rock rising from the 70m depths to just 29m below the surface creates a major obstacle to the flow of water that runs through here at up to 9 knots. It is reckoned that when there is a storm outside, the waves in this tide race can reach 30ft (9m) high. Combine this with the whirlpool and it is not difficult to see why the pilot suggests that the seas here can be very violent and dangerous and no vessel should attempt the passage without local knowledge.

V Kayakers enjoy the wild waters of the Falls of Lora.

We were routed through Corryvreckan on a Round Scotland race and, once again, it was mirror calm in the channel so I think we must have had charmed lives on that race, negotiating two of the most dangerous channels in the world without seeing anything at all to worry us.

Near to the Corryvreckan are the Falls of Lora that lie at the entrance to Loch Etive. This is a tide race that forms in the narrow exit from the loch when the water level in the Firth of Lorn drops below that in the loch. The water flows over a rocky ledge at the exit and spectacular rapids are formed at certain states of the tide, creating good sport for kayakers.

Japan has a major whirlpool that forms in a narrow channel where the Inland Sea in the south of Japan meets the Pacific Ocean. There is a strong flow of water through this half mile wide channel as the tides ebb and flow and the height difference between the two areas of water can be as much as 5ft (1.5m). The water in the channel reaches a speed of up to 10 knots and this generates a vortex that can be as much as 70ft (20m) in diameter. A huge suspension bridge across the channel gives a spectacular view of the whirlpool.

Some of the names say it all. In the Aleutian Islands there is Hell's Gate and The Race. Most of the channels between the islands feature boiling water of some sort, created by the ocean currents that run in and out of the Bering Sea. These currents can be exaggerated by the tidal flow, and this long chain of islands can be a challenge to small boats and the fishing fleets. Once again it is the wild water that seems to attract fish, and this region contains prolific fishing grounds, as in the Moskenstraumen area of Norway, which is noted for its cod fishing.

> *Once again it is the wild water that seems to attract fish and this region contains prolific fishing grounds.*

In the Strait of Magellan the strong currents that flow from east to west around the Southern Ocean try to force their way through the narrow channels inside Cape Horn where there are considerable tide races caused by the differences in height that can occur between the Pacific and Atlantic Oceans. This is noticeable particularly in the two sections of narrows that lie in the eastern section of the strait. Add the violent winds that occur in this region and the wild water can be dangerous for small craft, which may explain why sailing boats prefer to take the open ocean route around the Horn.

In historic times there was a considerable whirlpool in the Strait of Messina that separates Sicily from Italy but changes in this busy shipping channel have largely removed this, although considerable eddies can still be found. This whirlpool is thought to have been the origin of the Charybdis sea monster, the 'sucker down' that swallowed huge amounts of water and then blew it out again. Scylla was a rock on the other side of the strait and, with dangers on either side, this was the original 'between a rock and a hard place'.

To complete this chapter of wild water some mention should be made of tidal bores, waves that run up rivers at the change of the tide. These are found on many rivers around the world and are usually generated in tapering estuaries where incoming tides are funnelled into narrow stretches of river. It requires a high range of tide for the formation of a bore. The largest bore in the world is found on the River Qiantang in China where the wave can be a massive 30ft (9m) high and powers up the river at up to 20 knots. Such a massive bore is akin to a tsunami wave but, because it is predictable and regular, it is much less destructive. Large bore waves are also found on the Amazon and Orinoco rivers in South America, where the wave can be up to 12ft (3.7m) high, but nearly every country in the world has rivers with tidal bores.

Tsunamis

So far the storms and wild water in this book have all been created by the wind, tides and currents combining to form extreme conditions. However, there is a phenomenon that lies outside this category, one that is created when the earth moves. Tsunamis are the biggest waves in the world, waves that can be incredibly destructive. Most of the storm events described in this book so far can be predicted to a degree and there is even a growing knowledge about when extreme waves will be formed but tsunamis are almost impossible to predict, impossible to defend against and rare enough for people to become complacent about being caught up in them.

Because they only happen rarely tsunamis are not high on the list of natural disasters in people's minds but the Boxing Day Tsunami in 2004 reminded the public how these dramatic waves can sweep ashore and cause so much devastation. This one was caused by the movement of the Earth's crust below the surface of the ocean and it was notable because the location of the initial movement in the north-east Indian Ocean meant that the effects of the waves were felt over a wide area. Over 300,000 people were killed, many more than in any other natural disaster of recent times.

A coasting ship cast ashore by the power of a tsunami.

Tsunamis are so different from normal ocean waves that they are not always easy to understand. How can waves that are so destructive when they reach shallow water or the shore cause hardly a ripple when they pass in the open ocean? The key to this mystery lies in

A rare photo of a tsunami coming ashore – most people are running by now.

the very long wavelengths of tsunamis, which can be around 100 nautical miles. Compare this with the wavelength of a normal ocean wave, which could be around 300ft (100m) and the difference becomes apparent. The longer the length of a wave, the faster it travels and whilst a regular ocean wave might travel at 30 knots, the tsunami could be rushing along at over 500 knots. That speed dramatically

The aftermath of a tsunami with fishing boats and a road tanker mixed up on the beach.

reduces the warning time for land in its path so that it is only land that is over 1,000 miles away where there is a chance that a warning might be effective.

The very long wavelength is associated with a wave that may be only 3–7ft (1–2 m) high, so the gradient is extremely shallow and the wave will pass unnoticed by ships at sea. When the tsunami approaches shallow water it becomes slower and is compressed. The speed may drop to 40 knots and the wavelength fall to 10 nautical miles but the volume of water in the wave remains the same so the only way this can be accommodated is for the wave to grow in height. Depending on the slope of the shallow water, it may take some time for the wave to grow as it slows and this might give some early warning. However, if there is deep water close to or right up to the shore the onset of the monster wave will be sudden and dramatic. In both cases the first signs will be the drawback, the sea receding from the shore and exposing areas of the seabed that are not normally visible. For those onshore this is a sign to run but the following wall of water will be travelling far too fast to escape unless there is high ground or high buildings nearby. After that there may be a succession of big waves and on low-lying coasts the waves can travel a long way inland. The sheer weight of the fast-moving water can do incredible damage.

Early warning systems are now in place around some of the oceans that are susceptible to tsunamis and these can give a few hours' warning. For boats and ships that are already at sea this early warning may give time to head into or remain in deeper water but this water needs to be at least 100m deep and three or four times that is better. Craft in harbour may have a chance if they put to sea immediately and try to ride out the wave but they will need to get into deep water pretty quickly so going to sea may not be the best option – they may be better off following the crowds to high ground and leaving the boat or ship to its fate. The trouble is that there will be no clear guidance about which will be the best course of action and it will be too late when the roar of the approaching tsunami is heard.

The word tsunami is Japanese and it is not surprising that a word in this language has come into common usage around the world because Japan has been the main country to experience tsunamis, with 195 recorded there. Some of these have originated from earthquakes close offshore and the warning of the approach of the wave may have been 15 minutes or less. Other tsunamis to hit the Japanese coast have originated much further afield and the waves from the Great Chilean Earthquake of 1960 travelled thousands of miles across the Pacific to strike Japan as well as devastating many of the Pacific islands. It is mainly earthquakes that create the most devastating tsunamis and these can occur both on land near the coast or underwater. It is the underwater ones that are harder to detect and in many regions there are now detector buoys established to give as much warning as possible.

Weaker tsunamis can be caused by landslides or volcanic action. The biggest volcanic tsunamis occurred when Krakatoa exploded and sent tsunamis across the Pacific but most events of this nature are less violent and cause local sea disturbances known as shock waves.

> **The biggest volcanic tsunamis occurred when Krakatoa exploded and sent tsunamis across the Pacific.**

In Alaska in 1958 a landslide at the head of Lituya Bay generated a wave that was reckoned to be 1,740ft (530m) high but it only affected the immediate area before it lost momentum and died away. Three boats were anchored near the entrance to that long and winding bay that fateful evening and began to pitch violently. The two man crew of one fishing boat were awakened by a roaring sound and the next minute watched as a huge wave crested towards them. Their boat parted its anchor chain as it lifted to the wave and then it dropped almost vertically down the other side. Those two survived, as did the crew of a second boat, but the third boat tried to outrun the wave and was capsized and lost.

> *Historically, tsunamis are reckoned to have been responsible for some major events, particularly the parting of the waters in the Red Sea.*

In that landslide it is calculated that 90 million tons of rock and ice fell into the head of the bay from a height of 3,000ft (900m). The broken trees on the opposite shore suggested that the wave there had reached a height of 1,740ft and, further down the bay where the three boats were moored, the trees were demolished to a height of 110ft (34m). The speed of the wave was estimated at being over 100 knots.

Historically, tsunamis are reckoned to have been responsible for some major events, particularly the parting of the waters in the Red Sea although it is hard to imagine that they would have parted enough to allow people to cross. Noah's flood could have been caused by a major tsunami that inundated higher ground although that does not explain how Noah got early warning of the event. The lost land of Atlantis may have been destroyed by a major tsunami but evidence is hard to find. Certainly there is evidence of tsunamis in the seismic instability of the Mediterranean region, and throughout history they have been relatively rare but devastating events.

In the future, coastal areas will experience more tsunamis arriving with little or no warning. These ultimate waves, the biggest on the planet, will continue to threaten these areas, notably around the Pacific rim, and although the early warning systems may give better notice of their arrival, they will not change them. Rather like storm waves, tsunamis are something that man may be able to forecast to a limited degree but so far there has not been any significant progress in protecting people from them – at sea or on land.

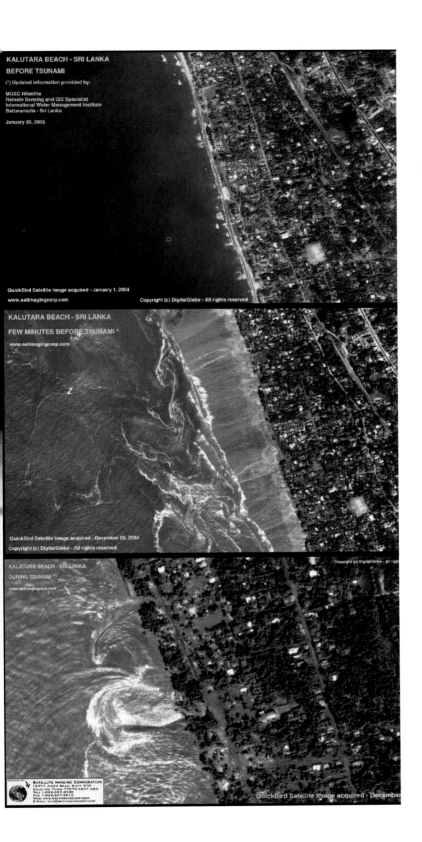

KALUTARA BEACH - SRI LANKA
BEFORE TSUNAMI

QuickBird Satellite Image acquired - January 1, 2004
www.satimagingcorp.com

KALUTARA BEACH - SRI LANKA
FEW MINUTES BEFORE TSUNAMI *
www.satimagingcorp.com

QuickBird Satellite Image acquired - December 26, 2004

KALATURA BEACH - SRI LANKA
DURING TSUNAMI *
www.satimagingcorp.com

QuickBird Satellite Image acquired - December

A series of satellite photos showing a beach before a tsunami, the water drawing back and then the tsunami powering in.

The Future

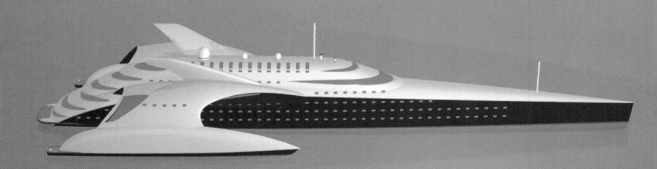

Man has tried to control most things in his environment but has failed miserably when it comes to storms and wild water. It seems that, for the foreseeable future at least, there will be violent winds and rough seas and shipping and yachting will have to learn to live with it. This is something of a worry because I can now see designers of these craft taking short cuts in the specifications and designs of their vessels that will reduce their ability to cope with storms at sea. The theory seems to be that with the accuracy of modern forecasting it is possible to avoid storms, or at least get advanced warning of their arrival. Ships and yachts therefore do not need to be built to the former standards for survival, despite the numbers of ships and yachts that suffer in storms and high winds. I find it surprising that insurance companies do not take a more proactive role in demanding higher standards.

The other approach would be to try to exercise some control over storms, perhaps to reduce their intensity and to release some of their energy. However, a tropical revolving storm can contain the energy of several hundred nuclear weapons, so any attempt at controlling this violent energy would be fraught with danger. It has not stopped scientists trying and back in 1969 the first attempts to 'seed' a hurricane were made. This seeding involved introducing silver iodide crystals, a similar technique to that used when trying to persuade clouds to drop their rain on parched soils. Hurricane Debbie was the first to be seeded in this way and the experiment was partially successful because the wind speeds in the hurricane were reduced by around 30 per cent. The seeding also released some of the energy stored in the warm moist clouds, the main energy source for hurricanes.

These early trials were not pursued but there is growing confidence that some form of hurricane control might be possible in the future. The focus of this control is on tropical storms because they are the most damaging and they are relatively compact. However, if you alter or divert a storm, the energy still has to go somewhere and so you could simply move the threat to another area. Any attempt to seed the destructive low-pressure areas such as those of the north

Is this the way ahead for the design of passenger ships capable of maintaining speeds in storm conditions?

Atlantic would probably be doomed to failure because of the huge areas involved. The present focus is on ways to reduce the intensity of these tropical storms but this poses the question of how to tap these huge energy sources. If only the energy in a tropical storm could be harnessed it would provide power for large areas of the world for a long time. When we look at the current attempts at generating renewable energy from wind they are insignificant compared with what could be available but there is not the technology available at present or in the near future that looks like coming anywhere near to providing a solution.

Wave energy could be a different matter but trying to develop machinery that can stand up to the destructive power of storm waves is a real challenge. It is much the same with tidal energy and, as we have seen in the Wild Water and Whirlpools chapter, the flows that might be suitable for this type of energy generation are often located in areas where the strong currents create challenging conditions for ships and structures. At present we tend to concentrate our research energies on trying to keep ships and boats out of these dangerous sea areas rather than trying to harness the power located within them.

There have been many gloomy forecasts about the results of global warming and how it will raise sea levels and make storm conditions occur more frequently. In my view there is a certain logic in this because most of the storms that occur around the world use heat as their main energy source. Heated air rises and cold air descends and that causes the flow of air rising and falling, starting off the wind blowing across the sea's surface. If there is more heat energy available through global warming the chances are that there will be a strong flow of air that will generate stronger winds. However, I am not convinced that this will happen because most of the strong wind scenarios that we see around the globe are caused by differences in temperature rather than increases in temperature. In the global warming scenario it does not seem likely that there will be any increase in the differences in temperature so I do not see an increase in the frequency or intensity of storms. This is incredibly complex and there are many conflicting views but I do think the early statistics that suggest an increase in storms and their intensity need to be taken with a pinch of salt.

> **Many think that global warning will increase the frequency of storms.**

Could it be that we are seeing stronger winds than we have in the past because we have better instruments to detect them and better ways of measuring them? Today a ship may be fitted with sophisticated wind measuring devices that can give an accurate picture of the wind strength whereas in the past a sailor might just have judged the wind by feel. It makes you realize just how little we still know about what goes on inside a tropical storm because there are very few actual readings taken at sea level. On ships the anemometer invariably gets carried away in storm winds because it is not designed to cope with extremes. Aircraft flying into hurricanes can take readings but these are not at sea level so the area where ships and yachts might get caught out is still unknown territory. When you are intent on survival you do not usually take instrument readings. You just know how bad it is. The regular non-tropical storms that sweep across the temperate oceans are now tracked with much closer precision and the wind strength in a storm can be calculated with much better accuracy, so the increase in quantity and quality of information could cause what appears to be an increase in storm activity and strength.

> **It is amazing how speed and seaworthiness have been combined in the current breed of round the world yachts.**

It is the same with extreme waves. Previously, the detection of huge waves relied on the verbal experience of seamen but now we are beginning to see measurements that can verify the enormous scale of some of these monsters. Before, extreme waves were measured by the damage they did. Now we have accurate measurements of the actual sizes of waves and we also have satellite technology that can help detect large waves in areas where there is no shipping. We are seeing what looks like an increase in extreme waves because the ability to detect them is improving. I suspect that they have always been there but the vast majority have not had any effect on shipping and have passed unnoticed.

What does seem sure for the future is that we are unlikely to see any decrease in storms. There is nothing in the weather patterns to suggest this and any attempt to control or moderate storms is a long way into the future. I also do not like the idea of scientists trying to dabble with the huge energy content of storms, which is like something out of science fiction – the 'mad professor' might get his sums wrong. A much more useful direction for future development might be to look at the types of ship design we need to cope with extremes. One solution is to have ships that are designed to go through waves rather than over them. Wave piercing designs are well known in the fast ferry business as a type that offers greater efficiency at higher speeds, but the same concept has been adapted to develop designs that offer a higher level of seaworthiness, with the ability to maintain speeds in rough conditions. At present the development of wave piercing monohulls and trimarans has been limited to small craft but designs have also been developed for larger sizes. The problem with these long slim hull shapes is that they lack internal volume and the space available to carry cargo or passengers is limited. This means that at present the concepts are not financially viable. A glimpse into the future can be seen with a huge 2,000-passenger trimaran design for carrying passengers across the Atlantic at speeds of between 40 and 50 knots. Technically it is feasible but financially it still has some way to go.

For yachts that go to sea for pleasure there should be no need for the ultimate in seaworthiness or speed but that would be to dismiss the requirements of the adventure or racing yachtsman. We seem to be at the peak of design with the current breed of round the world yachts and it is amazing how speed and seaworthiness have been combined in these designs. The hope must be for weather forecasts to improve their accuracy, particularly for forecasting extreme weather events, and giving better advanced warning so that storms can be avoided. The problem is getting those involved to concentrate on the dangers inherent in storms at sea and their consequences.

I will finish on a cynical note by suggesting that, if anything, ship design will focus less on being able to cope with storms and much more on carrying maximum cargo and passengers. In the case of yacht design the focus will be on developing ever more luxurious accommodation rather than optimizing the seaworthiness. Seaworthiness has become an old-fashioned, almost redundant word but the storms will always be out there waiting to catch the unwary, and we ignore them at our peril.

'Red Sky in the morning is the seaman's warning.' Within 18 hours of taking this photo a storm was raging.

Index